Designs In Patchwork

by Diann Logan

Oxmoor House®

To Mom and Dad with all my love.

Library of Congress Catalog Number: 85-61676
ISBN: 0-8487-0682-X
Manufactured in the United States of America
First Printing 1987

Executive Editor: Candace N. Conard
Production Manager: Jerry Higdon
Associate Production Manager: Rick Litton
Art Director: Bob Nance

DESIGNS IN PATCHWORK

Editor: Linda Baltzell Wright
Assistant Editor: Sandra L. O'Brien
Editorial Assistants: Lenda Wyatt,
  Margaret Allen Northen
Copy Chief: Mary Jean Haddin
Designer: Cindy Cooper
Illustrators: Cindy Cooper and Jane Bonds, whole
  quilt diagrams; Earl Freedle, patterns;
  Barbara Ball, assembly diagrams
Photographers: Courtland W. Richards,
  Cheryl Sales

Contents

Introduction

Quiltmakers have such a unique perspective on life. We look backward and forward at the same time. Behind us we see countless flashing thimbles, conjuring up everything from determined attempts to stave off the cold to breathtaking masterpieces done for sheer joy. Ahead of us, we recognize the distinct possibility that our quilts will outlast us, but we can neither predict nor control their fate. Will they be garage sale candidates, picnic blankets, or treasured heirlooms, fragrant from years in the cedar chest?

Each quilt we make is a bridge, past to future, ancestors to descendants. Our quilts become an avenue of self-expression and a chance to communicate to future viewers, as well as a link with those homey values we fear our society is losing: warmth, family, sharing.

This book is all of that for me—a look over my shoulder at my grandma and her friends around the frame, laughing and stitching; a look ahead to you, wondering if you'll like this quilt or that one, and what exciting things will happen when you add your interpretation to these patterns. Making the quilts was only half the fun. Sharing them with you is the other half. If you find something here that stimulates your imagination and gets you started on your first or next quilt, that's all I could ask for.

So come on . . . let's have a cup of coffee, and I'll drag a few things out of the closet to show you.

General Instructions

Yardages for Patchwork

All patchwork fabric yardages given in this book allow at least ¼ yard leeway. All are based on 44–45″ wide fabric. For that perfect fabric that is only 36″ wide, you will need to start from scratch and refigure the yardage needed. Don't use conversion charts in the fabric store; they are primarily for dressmaking and don't take into account the kind of layouts required for patchwork.

Fabric Preparation

All fabrics used in quiltmaking should be properly prepared before marking and cutting. Always wash your fabrics unless you are absolutely sure that the quilt will *never* be washed.

Washing the fabric will do the following: (1) shrink it, (2) remove excess dye and sizing, and (3) help square it up. *All* cotton fabrics will shrink, but exactly how much will vary from fabric to fabric. One washing will be sufficient for shrinking purposes. Use moderately hot water. In my experience, fabric isn't dirty when I buy it, so I don't recommend using soap or detergent. Two clear water rinses will do more than a soapy wash followed by a rinse. Never use fabric softeners, for they leave a residue that is quite unpleasant, if not downright frustrating, to quilt through.

"Excess dye" refers to dye that is lying on the surface of the fabric. The manufacturer has used more than is needed to insure maximum penetration, and the dye lying on the surface will readily wash off during the shrinking process. Red dye seems to be the worst for running and bleeding, so I recommend using either vinegar or salt to set the color. Add ½ cup of vinegar to the wash water or ¼ cup salt to one gallon of wash water. Let the fabric soak for 15 to 30 minutes and then continue rinsing until the water runs clear. It is best to set all fabrics containing substantial amounts of red, such as burgundy, bright orange, dark purple, hot pink, etc. As just a little further insurance, buy the best fabric you can find and afford. Cheap fabric for quiltmaking is *never* a bargain, and that is particularly true for red fabrics.

Marking and Cutting Fabric

Selvages are not used in quiltmaking, so either remove them or make a mental note not to draw to the edge of the fabric. If the fabric has been cut, tear one end to give yourself a straight edge. At this point check prints to see how straight the pattern is, relative to the grain of the fabric. If the pattern and grain don't match, you'll need to make a value judgement— how apparent will it be to the eye if the fabric is cut on the grain and the pattern is crooked? With most calicos and prints, it is hardly noticeable, but crooked stripes are a misery. The ultimate goal is to cut all pieces on the grain. Pieces cut off the grain will buckle, pucker, rumple, pull, or look stretched after the quilt is assembled. The farther off the grain they are cut, the more obvious these symptoms will be.

Here are a few suggestions to help you deal with off-grain printed patterns: (1) Learn to spot really troublesome fabrics in the store. Check striped and directional prints by looking both lengthwise and crosswise before buying. Make a lengthwise grain check by picking a point of reference in the pattern, and measure in from the selvage. Unroll the fabric one yard, pick the same point of reference in the pattern, and measure from the selvage. These measurements should be equal if the pattern is straight. Crosswise grain checks are made by following one thread across the width of the fabric, looking for pattern irregularities. (2) Be aware that you have a little leeway for compromise between pattern and grain line. (3) Beginners should make one quilt without stripes to become comfortable with the feel of fabrics cut precisely on the grain and to become aware of the need for accuracy in quiltmaking.

Press fabrics before marking, using a light steam setting rather than a hot cotton setting. The choice of a marking instrument is dependent upon the color of your fabric. For most fabrics a lead pencil is fine; for dark fabrics, a light-colored pencil, chalk pencil, or soapstone would be the best choice. Whatever your choice, the pencil must be *very* sharp. Ink pens or felt-tip markers contain substances that can bleed through the front of the quilt when washed and are not recommended.

Your touch for marking fabric should be as light as a breeze! Stroke the fabric with your pencil. The best description I can think of for this stroking technique is the way my mother showed me to apply eyebrow pencil—a series of short, light lines.

Begin marking at the straightened edge, tracing around the template shapes across the width of the fabric in rows, sharing common lines wherever applicable. In spite of all your efforts at perfection, however, it can't be achieved. Don't be surprised to see that your rows begin to slant upward as you work. As soon as this becomes evident to you, make another crosswise tear to give yourself a fresh edge.

Stay organized as you cut. Keep all like pieces together, in stacks, bags, or boxes. Nothing is worse than to near the end of piecing your quilt top and discover that one of your triangles has wandered off!

Suggested Cutting Layouts
Place squares across fabric in rows.

Place all rectangles except template 4 across the fabric in rows.

For template 4, place it across the fabric in rows on its short edge, rather than its long edge.

Place derivatives of rectangles across the fabric in rows, turning every other one upside down.

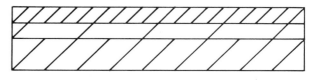

Place parallelograms across the fabric in rows, side by side.

Place rhomboids across the fabric in rows, turning every other one upside down.

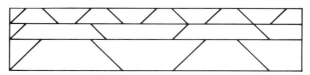

Place diamonds across the fabric, point to point. Templates 13 and 15 can also be drawn as squares. Templates 62 and 63 *must* be drawn point to point. Use the wasted fabric between them for cutting some of the smaller pieces. *Cinco de Mayo* is the only quilt that uses templates 62 and 63.

Place right triangles with two equal sides across the fabric in rows, always in groups of two that form a square.

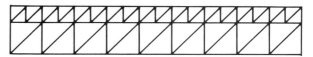

Place elongated right triangles with no sides of equal length across the fabric in rows, always in groups of two that form a rectangle.

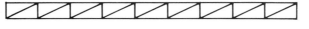

Place template 35 across the fabric in rows, with each piece touching the next, as shown. Ideally, the next row should fit into the first row, as shown. However, most fabric won't behave in an ideal fashion. In that case, start the second row fresh, and bring it as close as possible to the first row.

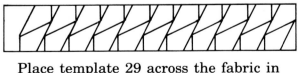

Place template 29 across the fabric in rows, always in groups of two.

One-sided and Directional Fabrics

Lots of calicos, prints, and even polished cottons are one-sided—that is, they have a definite right and wrong side. In that case, one-half of the pieces for some fabric shapes must be cut in reverse. This is accomplished by flipping over the template. The following templates need to be turned over as indicated, if you are using a one-sided fabric: 19, 20, 21, 22, 23, 29, 30, 31, 32, 40, 42, 43, 54, 56, and 60. However, it is always a good idea to give any new pattern a mental once-over to check for template shapes that might need to be flipped, even with the patterns in this book.

Pivot Points

A pivot point is used any time a piece is set in or a seamless piece is added to the edge that has already been sewn. The following principles apply for setting in, adding on, or joining an entire segment of a block:

1. A pivot point is always a three-step operation, involving three seams as shown in Diagram 1. The first seam is always the one to the right or top of the point to be pivoted around.

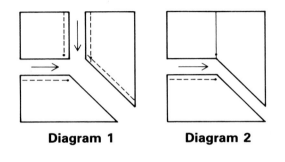

Diagram 1   **Diagram 2**

2. Sew the first two seams down to the dot (which is ¼″ from the outside edge) *toward* the pivot point, and backstitch one or two stitches—no more. (Diagram 2.) Big wads of backstitching won't enhance accuracy. They are a "no-no" in all machine piecing, but are especially pesky if they occur at a pivot point. It makes the corner hard to turn.

3. The last seam may be sewn in either direction. (Diagram 3.) A flap of material will form where the three seams meet.

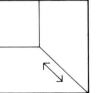

Diagram 3

At some point, what seems like a great inspiration strikes. "Aha, why don't I just combine seams 2 and 3? I'll drop the needle at the pivot point, turn the piece, and sew down the last side." In theory, this is a pretty good idea. In practice, it's just not as accurate. It may work perfectly about 50% of the time. The other 50%, you may have small puckers, tucks, and other unsightly "goobers" on the bottom side. Any square corners run the risk of not being square enough. While the errors themselves are small, the possibility of their occurrence is great.

Don't expect miracles. Perfect pivot points are more a result of practice than miracles. They are at least as challenging as a collar. Remember your first collar? I do! The motto for pivot points is: Don't stop now. More practice will pay off!

Continuous Bias Strip

Start with a square of fabric about 40–44″ on each side. Any smaller piece of fabric will cause seams to come around with greater frequency. Remove selvages. Finger-crease and cut the square in half on its diagonal (bias). (Diagram 1.)

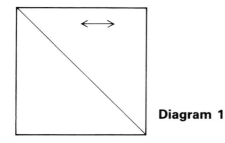

Diagram 1

Right sides will be facing each other. Join the edges marked Seam 1 with a ¼″ seam to form a parallelogram. (See Diagrams 2 and 3.)

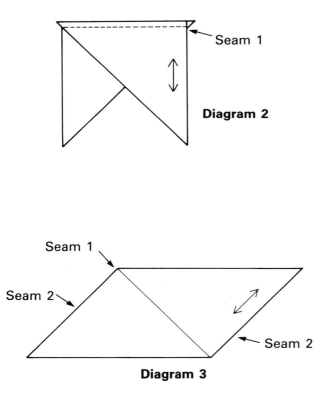

Join the edges marked Seam 2 to form a tube (Diagram 4), extending one end of the fabric edge marked Seam 2 by the distance of the width of the bias strip plus ¼″.

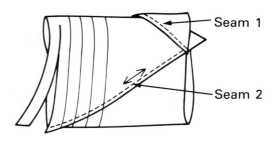

Diagram 4

Cut a continuous bias strip, beginning at the extended end and going around and around until the whole tube has disappeared.

Skill Levels

There really are no skill levels for quiltmaking. It just gets easier the more quilts you make. The skill level guidelines in this book refer mostly to pattern shapes and amount of quilting. The quilts designated *advanced* usually include very large or very small shapes, circular quilting patterns, and patterns that require greater marking precision. *Beginner* quilts contain simple shapes and only straight-line or outline quilting in moderate amounts. The main issue for beginners is to make sure the project is "finishable." What good is a quilt that can't be finished and ends up stashed in the closet for a decade?

But these gradation labels are just one woman's opinion. Gracious sakes, don't decide not to try a pattern based only on my level assessment. Experiment with one block. Use sale fabrics or old ugly scraps to practice any problem spots. Ask advice from other quilters. Lock yourself in your sewing room and don't come out till you've done a little patchwork, matched a few triangles, or gotten a kick out of exploring a pivot point. Don't be inhibited by my guidelines. Just use them to help with your decision and not to hinder your choice.

Flight of the Woofer

In stereo terminology a woofer is a big bass speaker. I married a stereo fanatic. The man's idea of fun is spending Saturday afternoon at a stereo store, listening to every woofer in the place and checking for subtle differences in quality of sound reproduction. (Early in our marriage I tagged along on these excursions, but soon discovered that once he was engrossed, I could sneak away for a few quiet hours and poke around in some fabric store.) None of our friends were surprised when I nicknamed him Woofer. Minutes after our daughter was born, her fate was decided. "What a precious Little Woofer," I sighed. I don't think the child knew she had a real name until preschool. By adolescence she was sick of

Little Woofer and demanded a more mature nickname. What else? Woofie! As for me, I've always been just plain Woof. *Flight of the Woofer* is a family quilt. We have all stitched on it. The open-armed windmill motif represents the freedom of the breezes and the spaciousness of life—things all Woofers thrive on.

Skill Level:
   Patchwork—Beginner (some bias)
   Quilting—Intermediate (large amount of straight-line quilting)
Finished Size: 80″ x 80″
Number of Blocks and Finished Block Size:
   16 Blocks—20″ x 20″ each

Materials:

COLOR OF FABRIC	YARDS REQUIRED	TEMPLATE REQUIRED	NUMBER TO CUT	NUMBER USED PER BLOCK
Brown Calico	2½	15	64	4
		52	256	16
White	5	2	128	8
		17	64	4
		19	64	4
		44	64	4
		52	320	20
Binding: White	¾	—	—	—
Backing: White Cotton or Muslin	5½	—	—	—

Block Assembly:
Each block contains 3 sections. Join pieces and sections as indicated by the diagrams. Make 16 blocks.

Block Sections

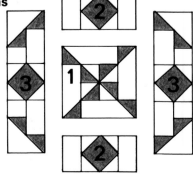

Section 1

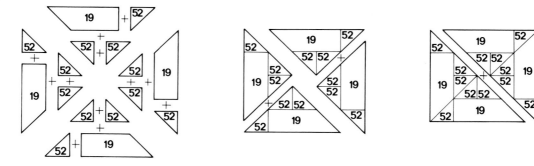

Section 2—Make 2.

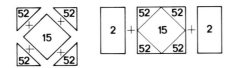

Section 3—Make 2.

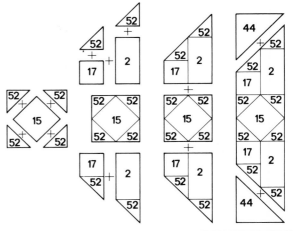

Final Assembly: Join Section 2s to top and bottom of Section 1. Rotate one Section 3, as shown, before joining to center column.

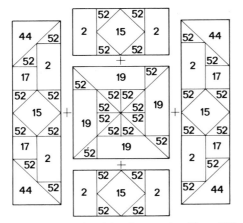

Make 4 rows of 4 blocks each. (See Whole Quilt Diagram.) Although the pattern has no top, the "right side up" of the block is determined by seam direction. Keep all seams marked by stars vertical in each block.

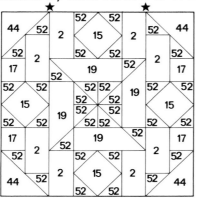

Quilting:
Outline-quilt ¼" from all seams. Horizontal and vertical parallel quilting lines are ½" apart.

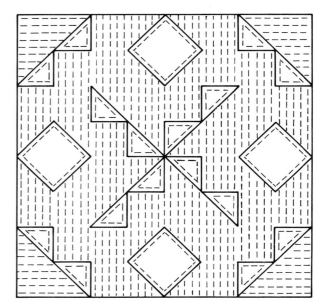

Finished Edges:
Bind raw edges with white fabric.

14

Rocky Mountain Bride's Quilt

The Rocky Mountains are vast and enduring. They weather many storms and at every turn delight the traveler with a new vista. So may it be with marriage. If a couple approaches marriage with a love that is vast and enduring, they can enjoy each new vista of the other, and weather the storms of life together.

Materials:

COLOR OF FABRIC	YARDS REQUIRED	TEMPLATE REQUIRED	NUMBER TO CUT	NUMBER USED PER BLOCK
Light Brown	1¾	58	128	8
Dark Brown	2½	42	128	8
		58	64	4
Blue	1½	16	80	5
White	4½	16	64	4
		42	384	24
		58	64	4
Joining Strips: Light Brown	*	16	40	—
Dark Brown	*	16	25	—
White	*	1	80	—
Border: Dark Brown	*	3" x 81"**	2	—
		3" x 87"**	2	—
Blue	*	16	52	—
White	*	16	52	—
Binding: Blue	¾	—	—	—
Backing: White Cotton or Muslin	6	—	—	—

*—Yardage is included in above measurement.
**—Measurements are given without seam allowance.

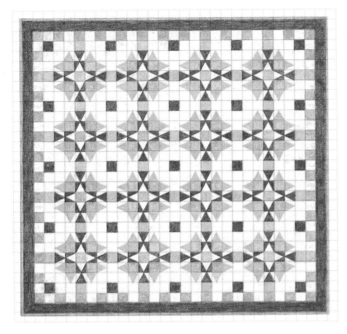

Skill Level:

Patchwork—Advanced (small pieces, triangles with very acute angles)
Quilting—Advanced (circles)

Finished Size: 87" x 87"

Number of Blocks and Finished Block Size:

16 Blocks—15" x 15" each

Basic Unit—This unit, using templates 58 and 42, occurs repeatedly, in various color configurations, throughout each block. (See Whole Quilt Diagram.) Make these units first. Each block uses 16 units.

Basic Unit

Block Assembly:

Each block contains 3 sections. Join pieces and sections as indicated by the diagrams. Make 16 blocks.

Block Sections

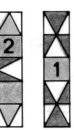

Section 1   **Section 2—** Make 2.   **Section 3—** Make 2.

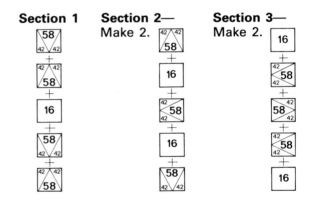

Final Assembly: Join columns, being sure to rotate Sections 2 and 3 as shown.

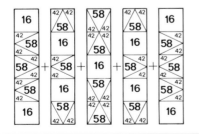

Joining Strip Assembly:

Horizontal Joining Strips—Make 40. Set aside 20 for use in constructing vertical joining strips.

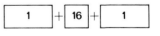

Vertical Joining Strips—Alternate 4 horizontal joining strips with 5 template-16 squares and join. Make 5 (shown horizontally because of space restrictions).

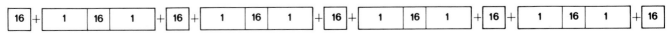

Quilt Top Assembly:

Row Assembly—Alternate 4 blocks with 5 horizontal joining strips as shown. Make 4 vertical rows.

Alternate 4 vertical rows with 5 vertical joining strips and join as shown.

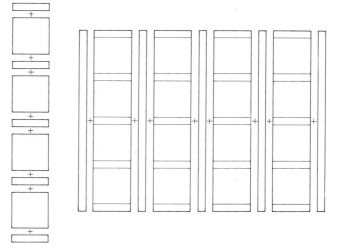
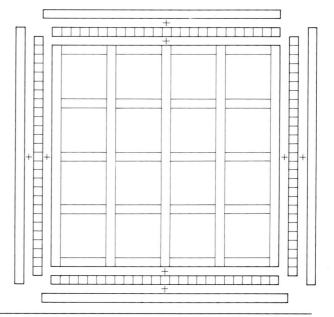

Border Assembly:

Horizontal Pieced Border—Join 25 template-16 squares, alternating colors as shown on Whole Quilt Diagram. Begin and end with a white square. Make 2 strips. Join to top and bottom of quilt.

Vertical Pieced Border—Join 27 template-16 squares, alternating colors as shown on Whole Quilt Diagram. Begin and end with a blue square. Make 2 strips. Join to sides of quilt.

Join the shorter, solid-colored border strips to the top and bottom of work. Then join the longer strips to the sides.

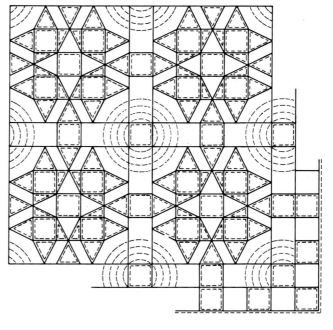

Quilting:

Outline-quilt ¼″ from all seams. The inner circle is 5″ in diameter. Successive circles are at 1″ intervals. Draw 4 circles. Solid lines indicate block segments and seam lines.

Finished Edges:

Bind raw edges with blue fabric.

Hobson's Choice

A fanciful story is told of one Thomas Hobson, a 17th-century stable keeper in Cambridge, England. It is unclear whether Hobson had more than one horse, but at any rate, it is said that he always required the customer who wanted to rent a horse to take the one that stood nearest the door. Either take that horse or no horse at all. These days, a Hobson's Choice is still an apparent free choice where there is no alternative. Be home by midnight or don't go out at all. Eat liver or go hungry.

Most of us don't like to find ourselves faced with a Hobson's Choice. We feel freer when we have some real alternatives. In the case of this quilt, though, maybe we can get some fun out of it.

In this quilt there are no alternate ways to set the blocks together. Whichever way you turn them, they still look the same. There are no ways to alter the border either. It only fits when the top is set in three rows of three blocks each. But if our *Hobson's Choice* doesn't appeal to you, you can turn the pages and explore other options.

Skill Level:
  Patchwork—Intermediate (joining of long bias edges of border)
  Quilting—Intermediate (large amount of straight-line)
Finished Size: 93″ x 93″
Number of Blocks and Finished Block Size:
  36 Blocks—12″ x 12″ each
Number of Units and Finished Unit Size:
  9 Units—27″ x 27″ each

Materials:

COLOR OF FABRIC	YARDS REQUIRED	TEMPLATE REQUIRED	NUMBER TO CUT	NUMBER USED PER BLOCK	NUMBER USED FOR BORDER
Brown	1¼	46	144	16	—
Pink	1½	16	9	1	—
		33	4	—	4
		46	128	8	56
		50	24	—	24
Print	1¾	6	36	4	—
		46	36	4	—
White	6½	1	60	4	24
		6	36	4	—
		16	72	8	—
		23	44	4	8
		24	4	—	4
		46	224	24	8
		47	24	—	24
Binding: Print	¾	—	—	—	—
Backing: White Cotton or Muslin	7½	—	—	—	—

Block and Unit Assembly:
  Each unit contains 4 blocks (Section 1) pieced with joining strips (Sections 2 and 3). Make 36 blocks, of which 18 will be the mirror image of the others. Join blocks with templates 6 and 16 as directed, to make 9 separate units.

Unit Sections

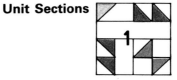
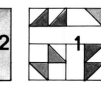

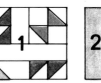

Section 1—Make 2 as shown and 2 the mirror image (MIR) of these for each unit. Arrow indicates top of section.

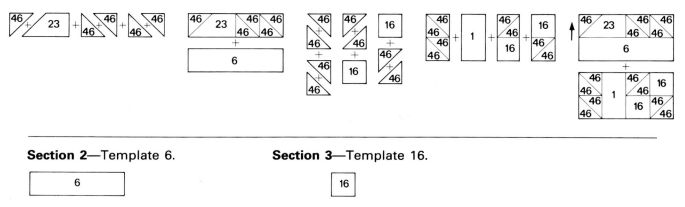

Section 2—Template 6.

6

Section 3—Template 16.

16

Final Unit Assembly: Form a column by alternating Section 1 with Section 2 and join. Make 2 of these columns, referring to Setting Diagram and Whole Quilt Diagram for proper section rotation. Join two Section 2s to Section 3 to form center column. Complete unit by joining these 3 columns. Make 9 units. Arrows indicate top of block.

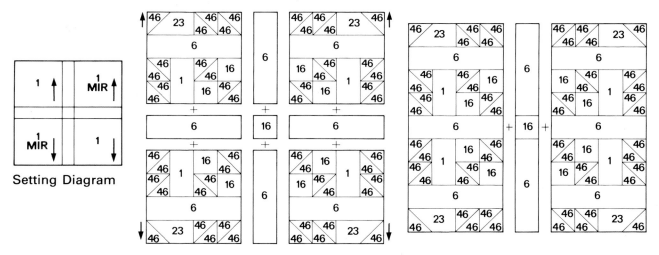

Setting Diagram

Border Strip Assembly:

Border strips are composed of 3 sections as shown. Make 4 strips. Corner blocks (Section 4) are attached to the ends of 2 border strips. Join pieces and sections as shown.

Border Section 1—Make 1 per strip.

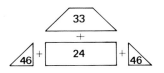

Border Section 2—Make 2 per strip. Each section contains 2 pieced triangles and 3 solid triangles (template 47).

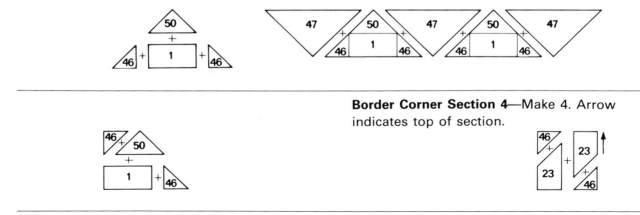

Border Corner Section 4—Make 4. Arrow indicates top of section.

Final Border Assembly: Join Border Sections 1, 2, and 3 in the following order: 3-2-1-2-3. Sew a Corner Section 4 to the ends of 2 strips, rotating them as shown in diagram.

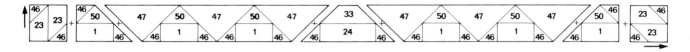

Quilt Top Assembly:

Make 3 rows of 3 units each, to form center section. (See Whole Quilt Diagram.) Sew the 2 border strips without corner sections to the sides of the center portion. Refer to Whole Quilt Diagram for proper border placement. Then sew the 2 border strips with corner sections to the top and bottom.

Quilting:

For Center Portion Blocks—Outline-quilt ¼″ from seams of triangles, and from seams of 2 sides of the white squares and triangles set around the pink triangles in Section 1. (See Quilting Diagram, which shows the lower right-hand quadrant of quilt.) For white squares only, quilt lines 1″ from outline quilting. Parallel quilting lines are ¼″ apart and ¼″ from seams.

For Border—Outline-quilt ¼″ from seams of all small triangles (templates 46 and 50). Parallel quilting lines within large white triangles (template 47) and corner parallelograms are ¾″ apart and ¼″ from seams. Quilt ¼″ from top edge of white rectangles. Quilt parallel lines ¼″ apart and 1″ from this quilting for each rectangle.

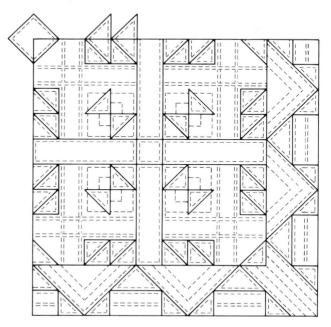

Finished Edges:

Bind raw edges with print fabric.

22

Blizzard

In Denver, lots of our blizzards are the tail end of storms as they move across the mountains. We often get to watch them break up as they head out to the plains. It's not unusual to see a foot of snow on the ground and a perfectly clear blue sky, dotted with the remnants of heavy gray clouds. This quilt is an attempt to capture those colors and express the exhilaration of seeing the blue sky again.

Skill Level:
   Patchwork—Intermediate
   Quilting—Intermediate (slightly complex snowflake design)
Finished Size: 90″ x 90″
Number of Blocks and Finished Block Size:
   9 Blocks—30″ x 30″ each

Materials:

COLOR OF FABRIC	YARDS REQUIRED	TEMPLATE REQUIRED	NUMBER TO CUT	NUMBER USED PER BLOCK
Gray	4	1	18	2
		30 extend to 8½″	18	2
		30F* extend to 8½″	18	2
		32	18	2
		32F*	18	2
		34	72	8
		46	72	8
		50	90	10
Blue	4	1	18	2
		30 extend to 8½″	18	2
		30F* extend to 8½″	18	2
		32	18	2
		32F*	18	2
		34	72	8
		46	72	8
		50	90	10
White	1½	12	9	1
		34	72	8
Binding: Gray	¾	—	—	—
Backing: White Cotton or Muslin	6	—	—	—

*—Flip or turn over template if fabric is one-sided.

Block Assembly:

Each block contains 3 different sections. Join pieces and sections as indicated by the diagrams. Make 9 blocks.

Block Sections

24

Section 1—Make 2 as shown and 2 the mirror image of these. Arrow indicates top of section.

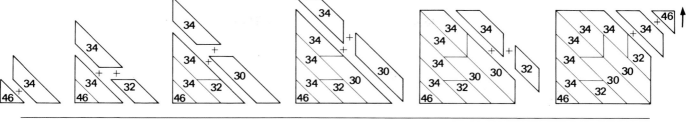

Section 2—Make 4.

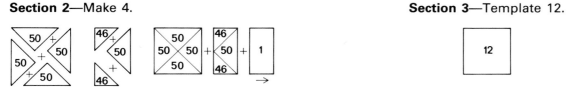

Section 3—Template 12.

Final Assembly: Join sections, rotating them as indicated on Setting Diagram. Make 3 rows of 3 blocks each, with each block set right side up. (See Whole Quilt Diagram.) MIR indicates mirror image block.

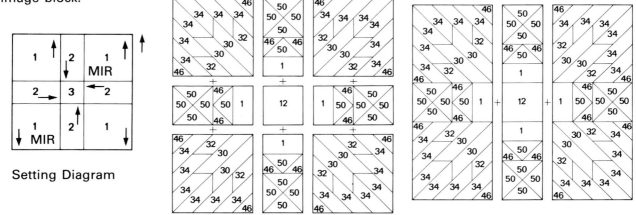

Setting Diagram

Quilting:

Outline-quilt ¼″ from seams as shown. Parallel quilting lines for the corners are ¾″ apart and ¼″ from side seams. Use snowflake pattern, found in Pattern Section, for Section 3 quilting.

Finished Edges:

Bind raw edges with gray fabric.

Crossroads

Crossroads make us think of an absolute either/or choice: one choice is right and the other, wrong. When faced with our own crossroads, an agonizing decision is often involved, because we want to pick the right one. But perhaps it is not always so. Perhaps there are some crossroads where either choice would be enjoyable—both roads lead to a desirable destination, or both landscapes are worth seeing. That is the case with this quilt. The choice here is only right or left, not right or wrong.

Skill Level:
   Patchwork—Intermediate (piecing of long bias edges)
   Quilting—Intermediate (large amount of straight-line)
Finished Size: 90″ x 96″
Number of Blocks and
Finished Block Size:
   24 Block A—15″ x 12″ each
   24 Block B—15″ x 12″ each

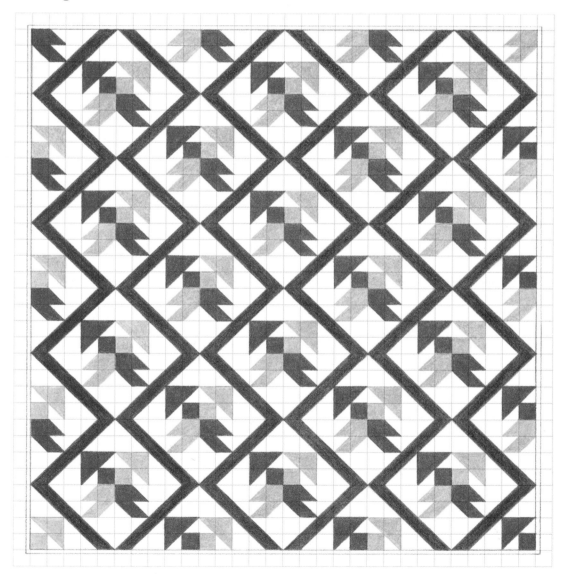

Materials:

COLOR OF FABRIC	YARDS REQUIRED	TEMPLATE REQUIRED	NUMBER TO CUT	NUMBER USED PER	
				BLOCK A	BLOCK B
White	5	46	240	5	5
		49	192	4	4
Dark Green Print	2¼	30 extend to 17″	24	—	1
		30F* extend to 17″	24	1	—
Peach	1¾	16	48	2	—
		32§	24	1	—
		46	24	1	—
		49	24	1	—
Green	1¾	16	48	—	2
		32F*§	24	—	1
		46	24	—	1
		49	24	—	1
Binding: White	¾	—	—	—	—
Backing: White Cotton or Muslin	6½	—	—	—	—

*—Flip or turn over template if fabric is one-sided.
§—Place template on right side of fabric.

Block Assembly:

Block A and Block B contain 2 sections each. Join pieces and sections for each block as indicated by the diagrams. Make 24 each of Block A and Block B. Two each of Block A and Block B will be required to form one large unit.

Block A Sections

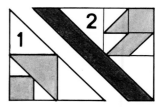

Section 1   **Section 2**

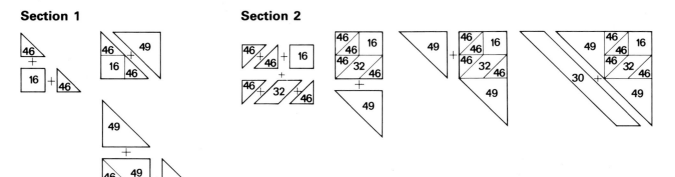

28

Join Section 1 to Section 2 to complete Block
A. Arrow indicates top of block.

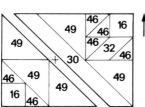

Block B Sections

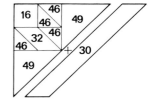

Section 1

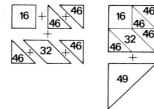

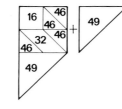

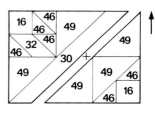

Section 2

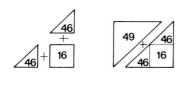

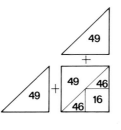

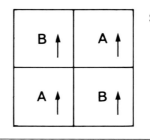

Join Section 1 to Section 2 to complete Block
B. Arrow indicates top of block.

Final Assembly: Join Blocks A and B into
units of 4 as shown, making sure all blocks
are right side up, as indicated by arrows on
Setting Diagram. Make 12 units.

Sew the 12 units into 4 rows of 3 units
each, making sure all units are right side up.
(See Whole Quilt Diagram.) Join rows.

Setting Diagram

B ↑	A ↑
A ↑	B ↑

Quilting:

Outline-quilt ¼″ from all seams as indicated by diagram. The checkerboard pattern is formed by perpendicular quilting
1⅛″ apart to form squares. Sections of
solid horizontal or vertical quilting lines
are ⅞″ apart. Dark lines on diagram indicate block seam lines.

Finished Edges:

Bind raw edges with white fabric.

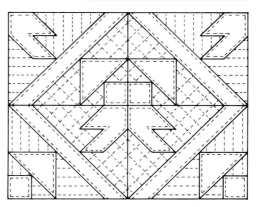

Cinco de Mayo

Cinco de Mayo (the Fifth of May) is a festive Mexican holiday, celebrated with joyful song, dance, and feasting by most Hispanic communities in the United States. Long before I knew the historical significance of Cinco de Mayo, I experienced many pleasant memories during Cinco de Mayo festivals. Eventually, my curiosity was stirred about the enthusiasm displayed by the participants. What was so special about the Fifth of May in Mexican history? Once I learned about the overwhelming defeat of the French army by an inspired group of Mexican villagers in 1862, I could understand the reason for observing this day. (A historical synopsis can be found after the directions.) I knew then I wanted to create a quilt that would embody the spirit of the Mexican celebration.

Skill Level:
 Patchwork—Advanced
 Quilting—Advanced
 Template Making—Advanced
Finished Size: 90″ x 96″

Number of Blocks and Finished Block Size:
 1 Block A—42″ x 54″
 2 Block B—Multi-sided
 2 Block C—Multi-sided
 4 Block D—55¼″ x 39″ x 39″ each

Block Assembly:
 This quilt contains 4 different blocks. Join pieces and sections for each block as indicated by the diagrams. Arrow on final assembly diagrams indicates top of block.

Block A contains 2 different sections. Make 1 block.

Block A Sections

Materials:

COLOR OF FABRIC	YARDS REQUIRED	TEMPLATE REQUIRED	NUMBER TO CUT	NUMBER USED PER BLOCK			
				A	B	C	D
White	5¾	1	8	—	2	2	—
		13	4	—	—	—	1
		22 extend to 9″	4	—	2	—	—
		26 extend to 12″	2	—	—	1	—
		26 extend to 15″	4	4	—	—	—
		28 extend to 12¾″	8	—	—	—	2
		33	20	—	—	10	—
		38	4	—	2	—	—
		39	10	2	2	—	1
		46	8	—	4	—	—
		47	10	6	2	—	—
		48	12	—	2	—	2
		49	16	4	—	6	—
		50	76	—	4	18	8
		60	4	4	—	—	—
		62	2	2	—	—	—
		64	2	—	—	1	—
		65	4	—	—	—	1
		66	4	—	—	—	1
Turquoise	4	46	4	—	—	—	1
		47	6	2	—	2	—
		50	102	—	3	26	11
		63	6	—	1	—	1
		64	2	2	—	—	—
		65	6	6	—	—	—
Green	½	47	4	4	—	—	—
		50	16	—	6	—	1
Binding: Turquoise	¾	—	—	—	—	—	—
Backing: White Cotton or Muslin	6½	—	—	—	—	—	—

Section 1—Make 2.

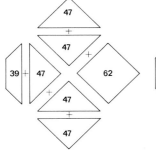

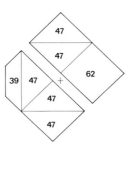

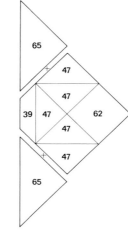

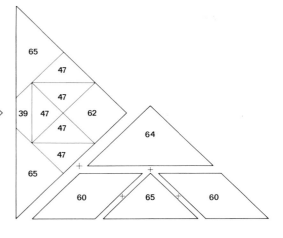

Section 2—Make 2.

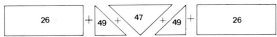

Final Assembly: Join Section 1s first. Join Section 2s, rotating one as shown.

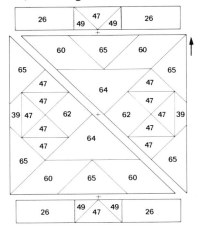

Section 2—Make 2, with 1 the mirror image of the other.

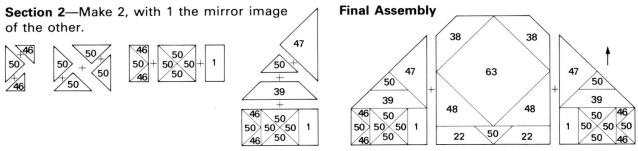

Block B contains 2 different sections. Make 2 blocks.

Block B Sections

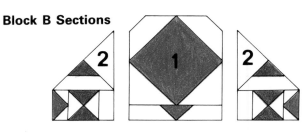

Section 1

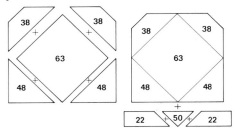

Final Assembly

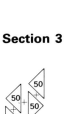

Block C contains 4 sections. Make 2 blocks.

Block C Sections

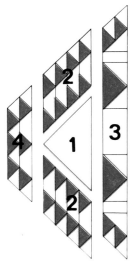

Section 1—Template 64.

Section 2—Make 2, with 1 the mirror image of the other.

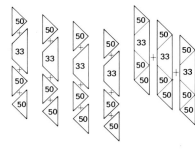

Section 3

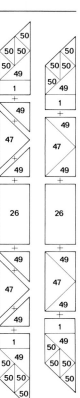

Section 4

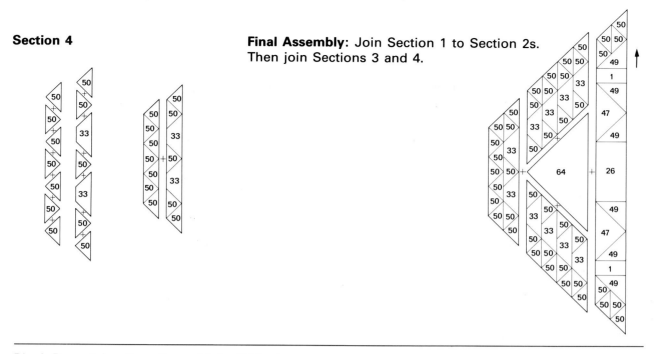

Final Assembly: Join Section 1 to Section 2s.
Then join Sections 3 and 4.

Block D contains 5 sections. Make 2 blocks
as shown, and 2 blocks the mirror image
of these.

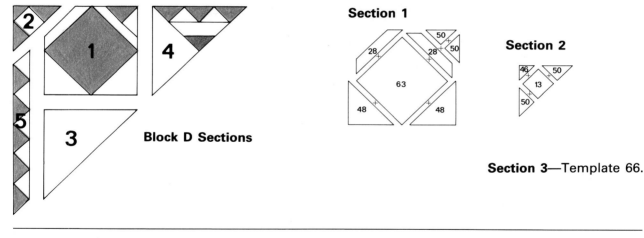

Block D Sections

Section 1

Section 2

Section 3—Template 66.

Section 4

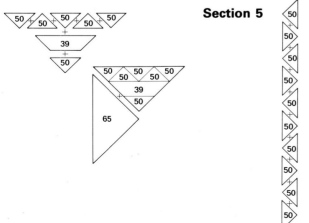

Section 5

Final Assembly: Join Section 3 to Section 1.
Join Sections 4 and 5, and then Section 2.

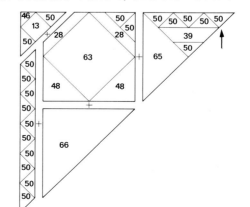

33

Quilt Top Assembly:

Join Blocks B and C to Block A, rotating blocks as indicated by arrow direction. Join Block D, rotating as indicated by arrow direction. MIR indicates mirror image block. (See Whole Quilt Diagram.)

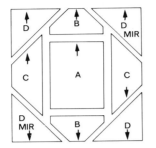

Quilting:

Diagram shows the top left corner of the quilt. Darker lines indicate block seams, so all blocks are shown. For the background, parallel quilting lines, 2″ apart, run diagonally across the entire quilt.

For Block A, parallel quilting lines in triangles (templates 65 and 64) are 1″ apart. Parallel quilting lines in the triangle at the top of the block are ¾″ apart. The remaining triangle begins with one set of parallel quilting lines ¾″ apart and ¼″ from seams; the next 3 parallel quilting lines are ½″ apart, and the last quilting line, ¼″ from these.

For Block B, outline-quilt ¼″ from triangle seams. The middle triangle (template 50) contains parallel quilting lines ½″ apart. The large diamond (template 63) contains 2 sets of parallel lines, 1″ apart, 2″ from each other, and ¼″ from seams.

For Block C, outline-quilt ¼″ from triangle seams as shown. Parallel quilting lines in large triangle (template 47) are ¾″ apart.

For Block D, outline-quilt ¼″ from triangle seams. Quilt large diamond (template 63) the same as for Block B.

Finished Edges:

Bind raw edges with turquoise fabric.

About Cinco de Mayo:

Cinco de Mayo commemorates the Mexican victory over invading French forces at La Batalla de Puebla (The Battle of Puebla), May 5, 1862. Ostensibly, the French had come to Mexico to collect debts owed by the Mexican government. Once there, however, the French commander embarked on a strategy intended to implement a secret scheme of Napoleon III. The plan was to march to the capital, conquer the country, and install a monarchy headed by Napoleon's choice. The French commander was confident that his 6,000 men could easily conquer the small band of Mexican soldiers.

Ignacio Zaragoza led the Mexicans, armed with little more than machetes. He told his army, "Your enemies are the first soldiers in the world, but you are the first sons of Mexico. They have come to take your country from you." After three failed charges, the French retreated in a blinding rainstorm. The French plans to conquer Mexico had been delayed by a year.

La Batalla de Puebla stands as an emotional turning point in the fight for freedom. The Mexican victory inspired new courage and sparked fresh resistance to any foreign domination of Mexico.

Breakfast at Zips

Zips is the name of a now-defunct coffee shop with a cheery decor and a bustling atmosphere. My breakfast there was a learning experience. Some of us weren't listening to what Mama said about the heartaches that come from pretend romances and casual flings. Learning the lesson the hard way was bitter, to be sure, but the brownies at Zips were still magnificent!

Skill Level:
  Patchwork—Beginner to Intermediate (lots of bias)
  Quilting—Beginner (outline and straight-line)
Finished Size: 50″ x 56″
Number of Blocks and Finished Block Size:
  20 Blocks—10″ x 14″ each

Materials:

COLOR OF FABRIC	YARDS REQUIRED	TEMPLATE REQUIRED	NUMBER TO CUT	NUMBER USED PER BLOCK
Blue	1½	53	20	1
		55	20	1
		56	20	1
Yellow	¾	3	40	2
		18	40	2
Blue Print	1	3	20	1
		14	20	1
		18	20	1
White	1¾	45	40	2
		53	120	6
		56	20	1
Binding: Blue Print	⅝	—	—	—
Backing: White Cotton or Muslin	3¼	—	—	—

Block Assembly:

Each block contains 5 sections. Join pieces and sections as indicated by the diagrams. Make 20 blocks.

Block Sections

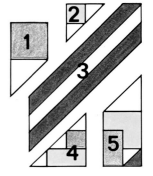

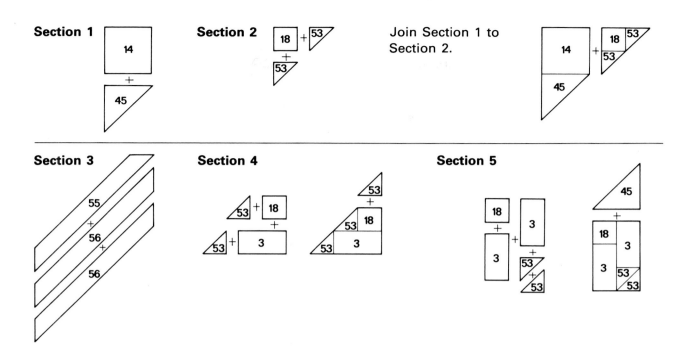

Section 1 14 + 45

Section 2 18 + 53 + 53

Join Section 1 to Section 2. 14 + 18 53 53 45

Section 3 55 + 56 + 56

Section 4 53 + 18 + 53 + 3 | 53 + 53 18 53 3

Section 5 18 + 3 / 3 + 53 + 53 | 45 + 18 3 / 3 53 53

Join Section 4 to Section 5.

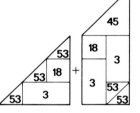

45 / 53 18 / 53 18 / 53 3 + 18 3 3 53 53

Final Assembly: Join large triangle formed by Sections 4 and 5 to Section 3. Join this to triangle formed by Sections 1 and 2.

Make 4 rows of 5 blocks each, making sure to keep each block right side up as indicated by the arrow on Sectional Diagram. (See Whole Quilt Diagram.) Join rows.

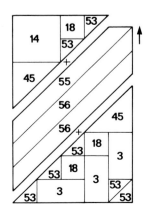

Quilting:

Outline-quilt ¼″ from all seams. Triangle 45 contains vertical quilting lines ½″ apart. (See Quilting Diagram.)

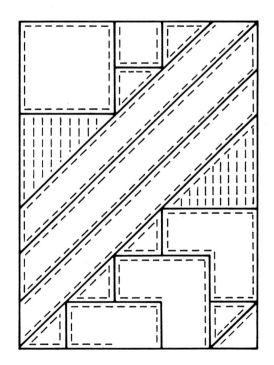

Finished Edges:

Bind raw edges with blue print fabric.

Cross of the Dunes

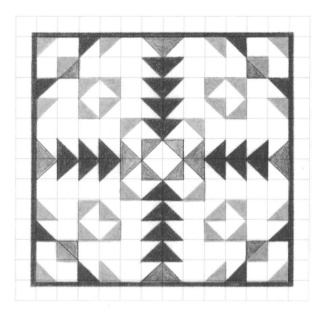

This is a "geography" quilt, a vision of a panorama of sand dunes. Imagine standing on the top of one dune. Every way you turn, dunes stretch into the distance as far as you can see.

This is a wonderful quilt for a beginner. The patchwork contains simple piecing, and there's enough quilting to make a beginning quilter proud of a beautiful wall hanging and to let her have fun too.

Skill Level:
Patchwork—Beginner
Quilting—Beginner
Finished Size: 36″ x 36″
Number of Blocks: 1

Materials:

COLOR OF FABRIC	YARDS REQUIRED	TEMPLATE REQUIRED	NUMBER TO CUT
Pink	½	46	36
Maroon	½	46	8
		50	14
Print	½	46	8
		50	6
White	1¾	1	8
		13	1
		16	4
		23	36
		46	28
		50	8
Binding: Maroon	½	—	—
Backing: White Cotton or Muslin	1¼	—	—

Block Assembly:

There is only one large block for this quilt, composed of the 3 different sections as indicated by the diagram.

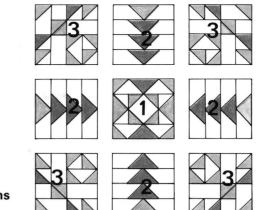

Block Sections

Section 1—Center Section. Make 1. Arrow indicates top of section.

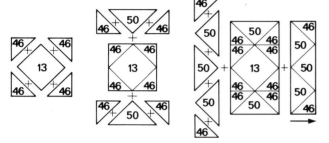

Section 2—Side Sections. Make 4. Arrow indicates top of section.

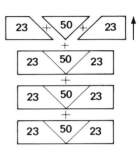

Section 3—Corner Sections. Make 4. Arrow indicates top of section.

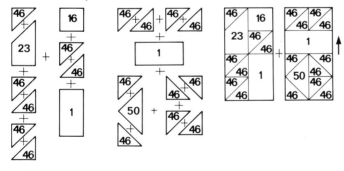

Final Assembly: Join sections into 3 rows and join rows. Use Setting Diagram and Whole Quilt Diagram for directional placement of side and corner sections.

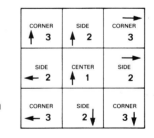

Setting Diagram

Quilting:

Portion shown on Quilting Diagram is the lower left-hand corner of quilt. Outline-quilt *all* triangles ¼″ from seams. For Section 1, quilt ¾″ from seams of the 5 diamonds. For Section 2, parallel quilting lines are ¾″ apart and ¾″ from triangle seams. For Section 3, parallel quilting lines are ½″ apart and ¼″ from seams. Quilting lines within white area enclosed by triangles are ¾″ from seams. Quilt a straight line from corners of Section 1 to center of triangle in Section 3.

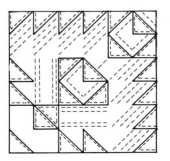

Finished Edges:
Bind raw edges with maroon fabric.

39

Grandma's Prairie Star

Lucky me! I had two absolutely perfect grandmas. One of them was a quilter, made the world's best orange chiffon cake, and taught me my first tongue-twister: "A big black bug bit a big black bear." Her influence in my life is obvious in the pages of this book. This quilt is for the other grandma—the one who always let me snoop through her purse, taught me to peel a boiled egg, made the world's best noodles, and was absolutely fearless when catching and killing the chicken destined to go with the noodles. Grandma spent the last years of her life on her daughter and son-in-law's farm in central Kansas. She could sit in her rocker on the wide screened porch and look out over a vast panorama of blue skies, wheat fields, the highway to town, the hen house, and—what else? Sunflowers.

In celebration of love and family ties, in recognition of the sacrifices made to keep Grandma at home instead of in a nursing home, and in fond memory of that beloved Grandma, I made *Grandma's Prairie Star*.

Block Assembly:

Each block contains 5 sections. Join pieces and sections as indicated by the diagrams. Make 9 blocks.

Skill Level:
    Patchwork—Intermediate
    Quilting—Intermediate
Finished Size: 90″ x 90″
Number of Blocks and
Finished Block Size:
    9 Blocks—24″ x 24″ each

Section 1

Section 2—Make 4.

Section 3—Make 4.

Section 4—Make 2.

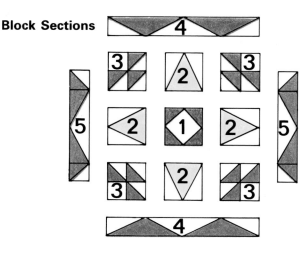

Block Sections

Section 5—Make 2.

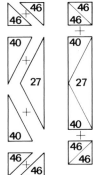

Final Assembly: Join, rotating sections as shown. Arrow indicates top of block.

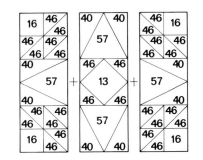

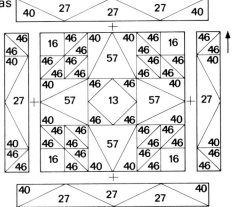

Materials:

COLOR OF FABRIC	YARDS REQUIRED	TEMPLATE REQUIRED	NUMBER TO CUT	NUMBER USED PER BLOCK
Blue	2¾	27	36	4
		40	18	2
		40F*	18	2
		46	144	16
Yellow	1	57	36	4
Brown	½	46	36	4
White	5½	13	9	1
		16	36	4
		27	36	4
		40	108	12
		46	144	16
Joining Strips: White	**	3″ x 24″***	6	—
		3″ x 78″***	2	—
Border Strips: Blue	**	3″ x 84″***	2	—
		3″ x 90″***	2	—
White	**	3″ x 78″***	2	—
		3″ x 84″***	2	—
Binding: White	¾	—	—	—
Backing: White Cotton or Muslin	6	—	—	—

*—Flip or turn over template if fabric is one-sided.

**—Yardage is included in above measurement.

***—Measurements are given without seam allowance.

Quilt Top Assembly:

Row Assembly—Join blocks to joining strips as shown. Make 3 rows.

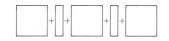

Join rows to 78″ joining strips as shown.

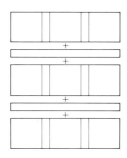

Border Assembly—Join 78″ border strips to top and bottom, and then white 84″ strips to sides. Join blue 84″ strips to top and bottom, and then 90″ strips to sides. Refer to Whole Quilt Diagram.

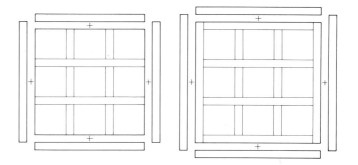

Quilting:

Outline-quilt ¼″ from seams of border strips, brown triangles in Section 1, white triangles in Section 3, and blue triangles in Section 4 and Section 5.

For Section 1, draw a circle 3½″ in diameter. (Hint: try a champagne glass.) Crosshatch lines are ½″ apart within this circle. (Hint: draw an X through the center of the circle first. Then measure lines ½″ to each side of the arms of the X.)

For yellow triangles in Section 2, use arc-shaped patterns in Pattern Section.

Parallel lines quilted on the white fabric between the yellow and blue triangles of Sections 2 and 3 are 1″ apart and ¼″ from seams of yellow triangles.

Parallel lines that form right angles in the corners are quilted ¾″ apart and ¼″ from seams.

For joining strips, use V-shaped pattern found in Pattern Section. Transfer to each *joining* strip, once with Vs pointing to the left and once pointing to the right, so that a diamond forms in the center of joining strip of each block. This pattern should repeat 3 times per row on the horizontal joining strips and 3 times per row on the vertical joining strips.

Refer to Quilting Diagram before marking fabric for quilting.

Finished Edges:

Bind raw edges with white fabric.

Love Is a Two-Way Street

Love is not a commodity—to be exchanged between partners like roommates swapping clothes. Neither can love be measured and stored in the bank like money. Swappers and bankers tend to think in terms of borrowing and lending. But love is not to be borrowed or lent. Love is to be given and received.

In choosing blue and pink, the symbolic colors for masculine and feminine, I was making a statement about the relationship between man and woman. So this would be a good wedding quilt. But the concept of interconnectedness would be equally at home in any other relationship and any other color scheme.

Materials:

COLOR OF FABRIC	YARDS REQUIRED	TEMPLATE REQUIRED	NUMBER TO CUT	NUMBER USED PER	
				BLOCK A	BLOCK B
Pink	3¼	28 extend to 12¾"	50	2	2
		32	25	1	1
		32F*	25	1	1
		49	50	2	2
Blue	3¼	28 extend to 12¾"	50	2	2
		32	25	1	1
		32F*	25	1	1
		49	50	2	2
White	3¾	32	50	2	2
		32F*	50	2	2
		47	50	2	2
		50	50	2	2
Binding: Pink	¾	—	—	—	—
Backing: White Cotton or Muslin	6	—	—	—	—

*—Flip or turn over template if fabric is one-sided.

Skill Level:

Patchwork—Beginner to Intermediate
(long bias sides of triangles)
Quilting—Beginner (outline and
straight-line)

Finished Size: 90″ x 90″

**Number of Blocks and
Finished Block Size:**

15 Block A—18″ x 18″ each
10 Block B—18″ x 18″ each

Block Assembly:

Blocks A and B use exactly the same
pieces, but the piecing configuration is
different. Join pieces and sections for each
block as indicated by the diagrams. Make
15 of Block A and 10 of Block B.

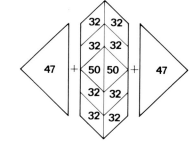

**Block A
Sections**

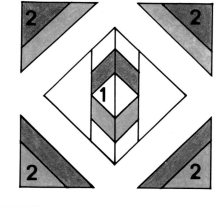

Section 1

Section 2—Make 4.

Join one Section 2 to each side of Section 1,
rotating each section as shown.

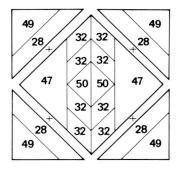

45

Block B Sections

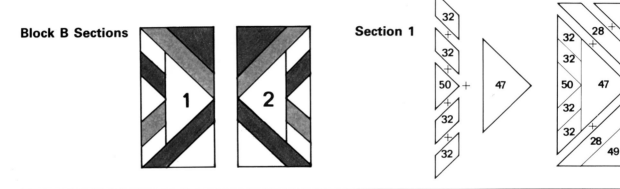

Section 1

Section 2—This is the mirror image of Section 1.

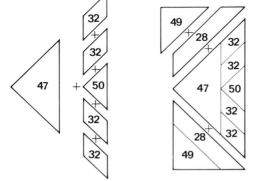

Join Section 1 to Section 2 to complete Block B.

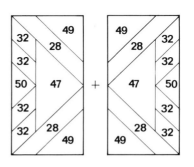

Final Assembly: Join 15 Block A into 3 rows of 5 blocks each. Join 10 Block B into 2 rows of 5 blocks each. Assemble so that Rows 1, 3, and 5 are Block A, and Rows 2 and 4 are Block B. (See Whole Quilt Diagram.)

Block Setting Diagram

A	A	A	A	A
B	B	B	B	B
A	A	A	A	A
B	B	B	B	B
A	A	A	A	A

Quilting:

For the inside white square, quilt parallel lines ½″ apart and ¼″ from seams. For the white area surrounding the chevron shape, quilt ¾″ from seams of the outer blue and rose strips and ¾″ from the bias seam line of the blue and rose chevron strips. (See Quilting Diagram.) For outside blue and rose triangles, quilt parallel lines ¾″ apart and ¼″ from triangle base seam line. Quilt ¼″ inside seam lines of blue and rose chevron strips and blue and rose strips at the base of outside triangles.

Finished Edges:

Bind raw edges with pink fabric.

Anniversary

This quilt is for my mother. *Anniversary* refers to more than just wedding anniversaries. Most families have their own special days—not just national holidays, but customs like marking the first snowfall of each winter with molasses cookies. Generally, it is the women—the moms, grandmas, and daughters—who keep track of this family calendar and remember these anniversaries. Each year of family life creates a circle of feelings as those anniversaries and traditions are repeated. For my mom and all moms who have kept the circle going through the centuries—this quilt is for you.

Skill Level:
    Patchwork—Advanced
    Quilting—Advanced
Finished Size: 84″ x 84″
Number of Blocks and
Finished Block Size:
    16 Blocks—21″ x 21″ each

Block Assembly:

Each block contains 8 sections. Join pieces and sections as indicated by the diagrams. Make 16 blocks.

Block Sections

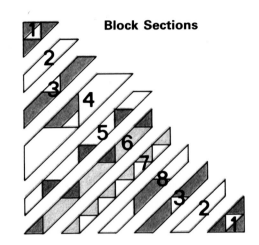

Materials:

COLOR OF FABRIC	YARDS REQUIRED	TEMPLATE REQUIRED	NUMBER TO CUT	NUMBER USED PER BLOCK
Navy	1¼	46	176	11
Brown	1¾	34	96	6
		46	32	2
Print	1½	34	48	3
		46	96	6
White	4¾	28 extend to 12¾"	32	2
		32	32	2
		34	64	4
		38	32	2
		46	160	10
Binding: Navy	¾	—	—	—
Backing: White Cotton or Muslin	5½	—	—	—

Section 1—Make 2.

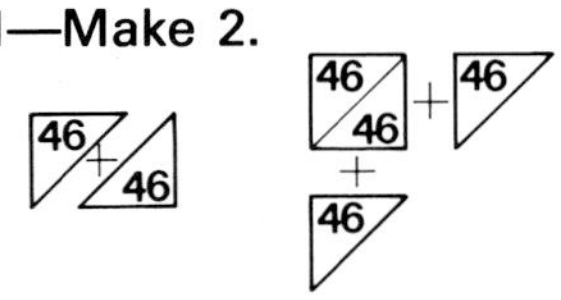

Section 2—Template 28.

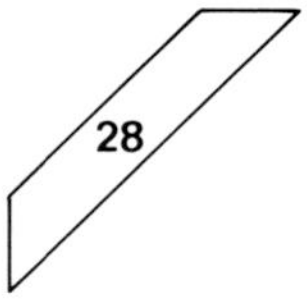

Section 3—Make 2.

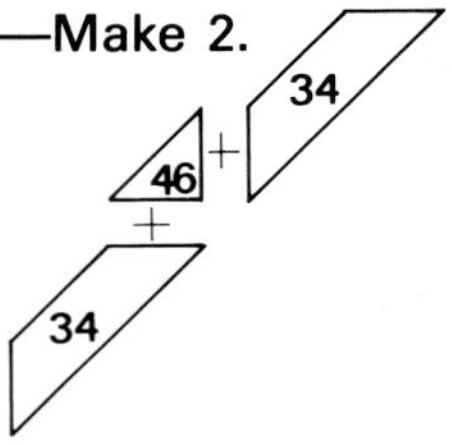

48

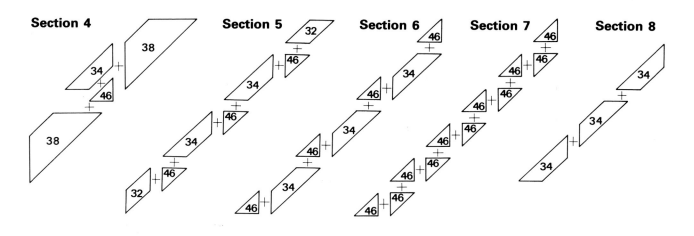

Section 4 **Section 5** **Section 6** **Section 7** **Section 8**

Final Assembly: Join sections in the following order: 1, 2, 3, 4, 5, 6, 7, 8, rotated 3, rotated 2, rotated 1. Arrow indicates top of the block.

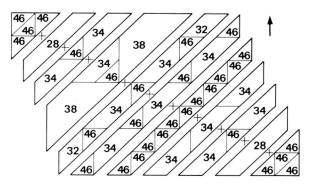

Quilt Top Assembly:

Join 4 blocks, rotating each for proper placement, as shown. This forms 1 unit. Make 2 rows of 2 units each. (See Whole Quilt Diagram.)

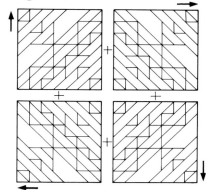

Quilting:

Outline quilting is ¼″ from seams. Parallel quilting lines in Sections 1 and 3 are ½″ apart and ¼″ from seams. Parallel quilting lines in Sections 7 and 8 are ¾″ apart and ¼″ from seams. Parallel quilting lines in Sections 4 *and* 5 are 1″ apart and ½″ from seams. Parallel quilting lines on template 32 of Section 5 are ½″ apart and ¼″ from seams.

Finished Edges:

Bind raw edges with navy fabric.

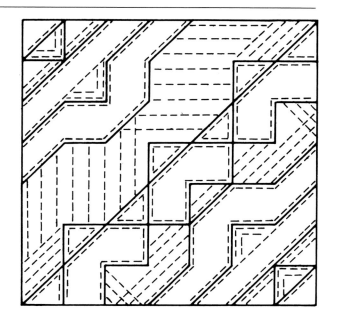

Waltz

This is a "musical" quilt, based on the three-quarter time of the waltz. With its patchwork and three lines of curved quilting, it tries to capture the whirling gracefulness of the waltz step. While quilting, imagine yourself in Europe when the waltz was introduced. The dance was considered immodest and certainly quite exciting since the partners danced so close. Whirling around the floor in the arms of a gallant gentleman could set a girl's heart all aflutter. These days the gallant gentleman who waltzes divinely is nearly extinct. If one should approach you, say yes (demurely) with lowered lashes and offer him your dance card!

Materials:

COLOR OF FABRIC	YARDS REQUIRED	TEMPLATE REQUIRED	NUMBER TO CUT	NUMBER USED PER BLOCK
Navy	¾	31	20	1
Gray	¾	1	20	1
Maroon	1	31F*	20	1
White	1	24	20	1
		46	40	2
Print	¾	33	20	1
Border: Maroon	**	3" x 45"***	2	—
Binding: Maroon	½	—	—	—
Backing: White Cotton or Muslin	2	—	—	—

*—Flip or turn over template if fabric is one-sided.

**—Yardage is included in above measurement.

***—Measurement is given without seam allowance.

Skill Level:

Patchwork—Intermediate (pivot points)
Quilting—Beginner (outline and curved)

Finished Size: 45" x 54"

Number of Blocks and
Finished Block Size:

20 Blocks—9" x 12" each

Block Assembly:

Each block contains 2 sections. Join pieces and sections as indicated by diagrams. Make 20 blocks.

Block Sections

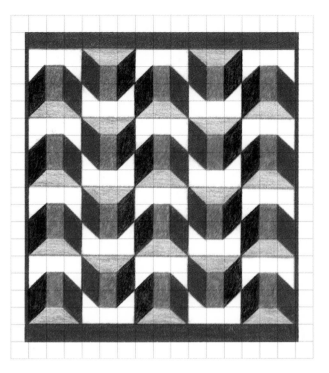

Section 1

Section 2—Stars indicate pivot points.

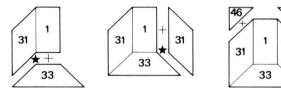

Final Assembly: Arrow indicates top of block. Make 4 rows of 5 blocks each, turning every other block upside down. (See Setting Diagram.) Join rows.

Border:

Cut 2 pieces 3" x 45", adding seam allowances. Join border to top and bottom of block rows. (See Setting and Whole Quilt Diagrams.)

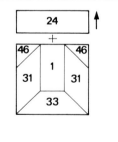

Setting Diagram

Quilting:

To form the curved band of three quilt lines, use a dinner plate to trace an arc ½" from seam line at top of block; then trace 2 more arcs ¼" apart below that one. Outline-quilt ¼" from seams of the solid and printed fabrics. Vertical quilting lines are ¼" apart.

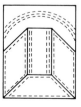

Finished Edges:

Bind raw edges with maroon fabric.

51

Twenty-Four Pointed Star

The inspiration for this pattern is a twenty-four pointed star that resulted from my participation in a casual exercise in geometry. I decided I wanted to use the basic shape found in this quilt pattern, but didn't know exactly how. While exploring different placements, I saw a star, counted the points, and surprise, a twenty-four pointed star! However, the design is not pieced in blocks of stars, but rather in horizontal rows.

This is a challenge quilt and should only be attempted by advanced quilters. The difficulty lies in accurately joining the basic unit. Give yourself every advantage you can at this stage. Mark the seam lines on the first dozen (or two dozen or ten dozen) of these units until you are quite familiar with what the seam allowances should look like from the back, at the corner where all the points come together. Also, take special note of the grain line direction indicated on the cutting diagrams. Prepare yourself for a long siege of only two colors and give yourself a well-deserved pat on the back when the quilt is finally finished. The end result is so stunning you'll be glad you invested the time and energy!

Skill Level:
  Patchwork—Advanced
  Quilting—Advanced
Finished Size: 90″ x 90″
Number of Blocks and Finished Block Size:
  100 Block A—6″ x 6″ each
  40 Block B—12″ x 6″ each
  10 Block C—6″ x 6″ each
  10 Block D—6″ x 12″ each

Materials:

COLOR OF FABRIC	YARDS REQUIRED	TEMPLATE REQUIRED	NUMBER TO CUT	NUMBER USED PER			
				BLOCK A	BLOCK B	BLOCK C	BLOCK D
Maroon	4¼	35	600	4	4	2	2
White	6¼	1	20	—	—	1	1
		12	65*	—	1	—	1
		42	1200	8	8	4	4
Binding: Maroon	¾	—	—	—	—	—	—
Backing: White Cotton or Muslin	6	—	—	—	—	—	—

*—Fifteen are used to make horizontal row 2.

Block Assembly:

There are four different blocks to make for this quilt. A basic unit is contained in Block A that is used in all other blocks, so begin with Block A. Join pieces and sections for each block as indicated by the diagrams.

Basic Unit—This basic unit is contained in all blocks. Though it's possible to die of boredom while piecing these, to save time make 600! Use 400 to make 100 of Block A, and set aside 160 for Block B, 20 for Block C, and 20 for Block D.

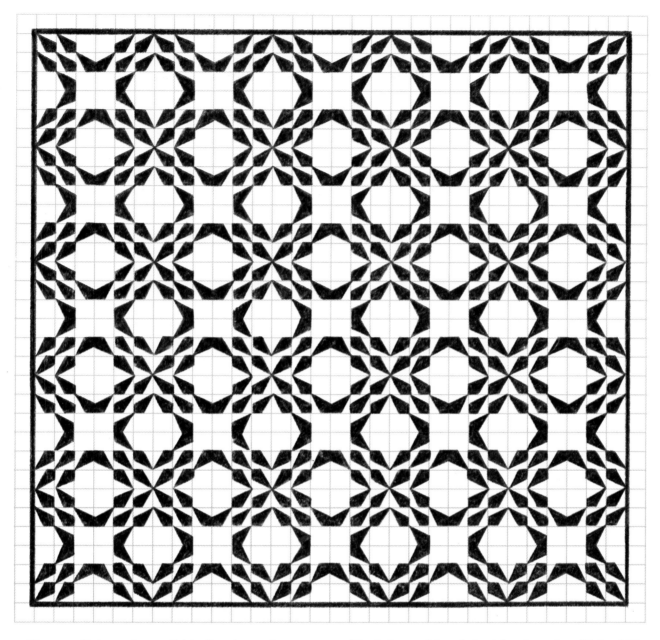

There will be substantial bulk where the three points meet, but do not trim any of it away at this stage. Any grading of seams should be done only when the entire top is completed.

Final Assembly: Join 4 basic units. Make 100 blocks. Arrow indicates top of block.

Block A Sections

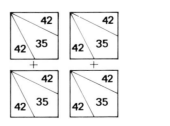

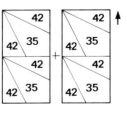

Block B Sections

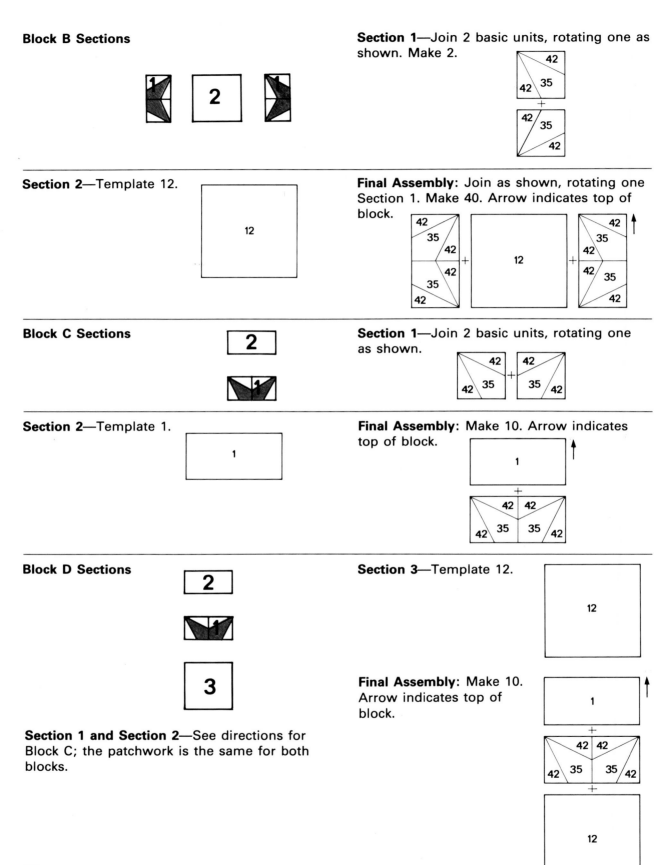

Section 1—Join 2 basic units, rotating one as shown. Make 2.

Section 2—Template 12.

Final Assembly: Join as shown, rotating one Section 1. Make 40. Arrow indicates top of block.

Block C Sections

Section 1—Join 2 basic units, rotating one as shown.

Section 2—Template 1.

Final Assembly: Make 10. Arrow indicates top of block.

Block D Sections

Section 1 and Section 2—See directions for Block C; the patchwork is the same for both blocks.

Section 3—Template 12.

Final Assembly: Make 10. Arrow indicates top of block.

Quilt Top Assembly:

For each horizontal row assembly, there are two diagrams: one illustrating the symbolic block usage and the other, a schematic representation. Each row should measure 90″ in length. Use directional arrows for top of block placement.

Row Assembly

Row 1—Use 10 Block A and 5 Block C to form a horizontal row. Make 2 rows.

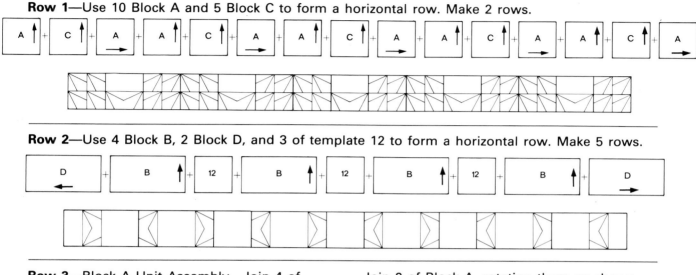

Row 2—Use 4 Block B, 2 Block D, and 3 of template 12 to form a horizontal row. Make 5 rows.

Row 3—Block A Unit Assembly—Join 4 of Block A, rotating them as shown. Make 4.

Join 2 of Block A, rotating them as shown. Make 2.

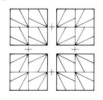

Final Assembly: Use 4 of the four-block units of Block A, 2 of the two-block units of Block A, and 5 Block B. Alternate the four-block units of Block A with Block B. Place the two-block units of Block A at each end and join. Use 20 Block A to form each row. Make 4 rows.

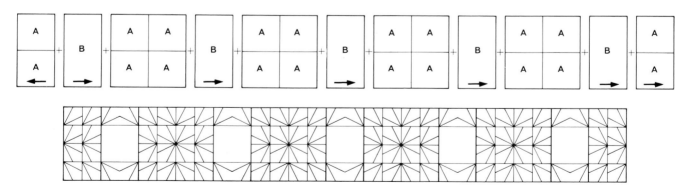

Final Assembly (continued): Join horizontal rows in alternating fashion as shown. Row 1 at the bottom is turned upside down. (See Whole Quilt Diagram.)

Row 1
+
Row 2
+
Row 3
+
Row 2
+
Row 3
+
Row 2
+
Row 3
+
Row 2
+
Row 3
+
Row 2
+
Row 1

Quilting:

Portion shown is the quilt's upper right-hand corner. Darker lines on diagram indicate row seams. From top to bottom this diagram illustrates Row 1, Row 2, Row 3, and Row 2. The small circles are reference points used to make the diagonal quilting lines. They are placed at seam lines and corners. All quilting is done on the white fabric. Outline quilting is ¼″ from seams.

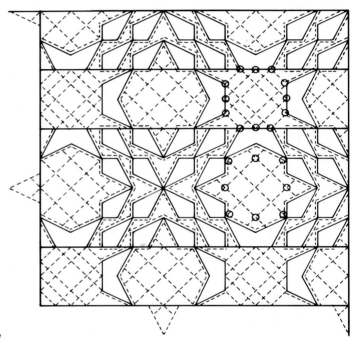

Finished Edges:
Bind raw edges with maroon fabric.

58

Caracole

Caracole is a rather fancy word for zig-zag. It refers to a prancing half-turn to the left, then a half-turn to the right, executed by a mounted horse. It takes quite a rider to stay mounted through this equestrian jitterbug.

Instructions and materials are given for a 54" x 54" quilt. *Caracole* can also be made into a lovely 90" x 90" quilt, as shown by the Whole Quilt Diagram.

Skill Level:
    Patchwork—Advanced (pivot points in every block)
    Quilting—Beginner
Finished Size: 54" x 54"
Number of Blocks and
Finished Block Size:
    9 Blocks—18" x 18" each

Materials:

COLOR OF FABRIC	YARDS REQUIRED	TEMPLATE REQUIRED	NUMBER TO CUT	NUMBER USED PER BLOCK
Green	1¼	22 extend to 9″	18	2
		23	18	2
Dark Turquoise	1½	30 extend to 12¾″	18	2
		32	18	2
		34	18	2
Aqua	1	28 extend to 12¾″	18	2
		46	36	4
White	1½	38	18	2
		50	18	2
Binding: Green	½	—	—	—
Backing: White Cotton or Muslin	3½	—	—	—

Block Assembly:

Each block contains 2 identical sections, with one rotated before joining. Stars denote pivot points. (See section on Pivot Points in General Instructions.) Make 9 blocks.

Block Sections

Final Assembly: Join sections as shown. Arrow indicates top of the block. Join blocks into 3 rows of 3 blocks each, making sure all blocks are right side up. (See upper left segment of Whole Quilt Diagram.)

Section Assembly—Make 2.

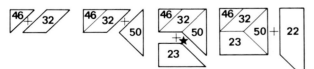

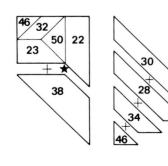

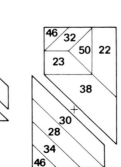

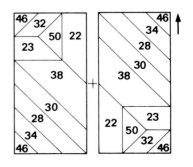

60

Quilt Backing:

Piece backing with one center seam. There will be excess fabric, but having one center seam is preferable to having several.

Quilting:

Outline-quilt ¼″ from all seams. Parallel quilting lines are 1″ apart.

Finished Edges:

Bind raw edges with green fabric.

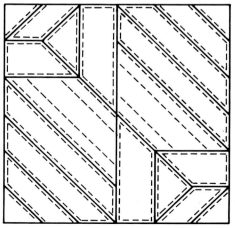

Ghost Dance

Sometimes a quilt "tells" you its name. The skeletal prairie feeling emitted from this quilt said *Ghost Dance* was a proper name. After researching other quilt titles and origins, I felt a responsibility to the name I had given this quilt. While talking with a woman from the Sioux Indian tribe and doing some reading, I learned that the ghost dance was a religious ritual performed by various Indian tribes throughout the United States. I became intrigued with the governmental politics involved with the dance and have summarized the dance and the events surrounding it below. The story may cause other quilters, as it did me, to recognize the responsibility entailed in the naming of a quilt.

Skill Level:
    Patchwork—Intermediate
    Quilting—Beginner
Finished Size: 90″ x 90″

Number of Blocks and
Finished Block Size:
    12 Block A—30″ x 15″ each
    12 Block B—15″ x 15″ each

Materials:

COLOR OF FABRIC	YARDS REQUIRED	TEMPLATE REQUIRED	NUMBER TO CUT	NUMBER USED PER	
				BLOCK A	BLOCK B
Gold	¾	46	72	—	6
Maroon	2	1	12	1	—
		16	24	2	—
		46	204	12	5
Print	1¾	50	120	10	—
White	6½	1	60	4	1
		16	48	2	2
		22 extend to 9″	12	—	1
		23	144	4	8
		34	48	4	—
		46	120	8	2
		50	48	4	—
Binding: Maroon	¾	—	—	—	—
Backing: White Cotton or Muslin	6	—	—	—	—

About the Ghost Dance:

The ghost dance was originated by a Paiute medicine man named Wavoka, who proclaimed that the Great Spirit had selected him to lead all tribesmen back to their old existence. J. Mooney, in a report to the Bureau of American Ethnology in 1896, explained that the ghost dance doctrine professed that "the whole Indian race, living and dead, will be reunited upon a regenerated earth, to live a life of happiness, forever free from death, disease, and misery." The oppression by the white man may have encouraged its frequent performance and the belief by many Indians that, by performing the dance, this happiness could be hastened into reality through the hypnotic trances that occurred during the dance.

Many tribes, including the Cheyenne, Arapaho, Shoshoni, and Sioux, adopted the ghost dance in their religious rituals. It was usually performed in the middle of the afternoon after a period of fasting. Dancers wore what became known as the "ghost shirt"—made of white cloth with no metal adornments. These shirts were supposed to stop the white man's bullets. Dancers would begin to chant, marching abreast, with others coming in behind as they marched. No drums, rattles, or other musical instruments were used.

The marching caused the ground to be pounded into a fine dust, which would often engulf dancers until they could not be seen. The chanting would continue until one after another would begin to collapse. Once a majority of dancers was lying unconscious, the dance would stop. Those lying unconscious were communing with the spirit world and could not be disturbed. As the unconscious dancers recovered, they would share their visions.

During the late 1800s the government forbade the performance of the ghost dance and many other religious celebrations by Indian tribes. The government feared these spiritual ceremonies would unify the tribes into a solid resistance against the westward expansion of the white man.

After the Battle at Wounded Knee and other conquests of the Indian by the white man, however, the ghost dance lost its validity for many Indians since the happiness it promised never came; and even the authenticity of the visions was questioned by tribe members. Many tribes continued to perform the ghost dance in secret, but expectations were much more subdued.

Block Assembly:

Make 12 each of Block A and Block B.

Block A Sections

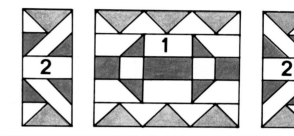

Section 1

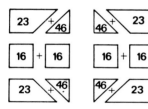

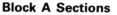

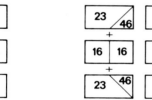

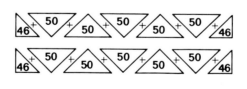

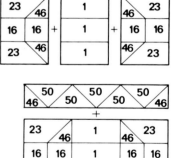

Section 2—Make 2.

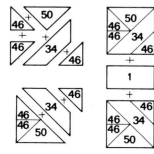

Final Assembly: Join a Section 2 to each side of Section 1, being sure to rotate one Section 2 as shown in diagram.

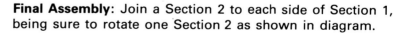

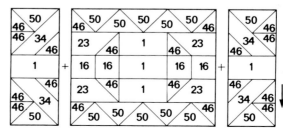

Block B Sections

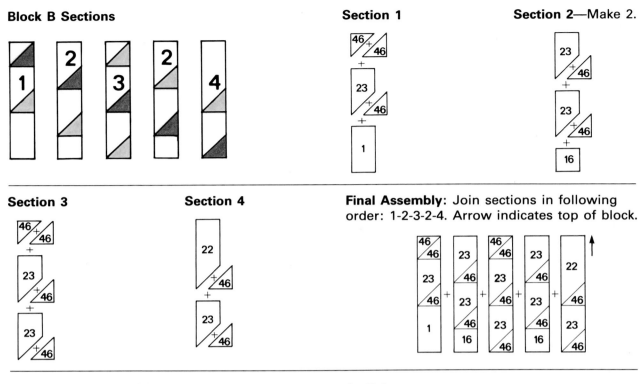

Section 1

Section 2—Make 2.

Section 3

Section 4

Final Assembly: Join sections in following order: 1-2-3-2-4. Arrow indicates top of block.

Quilt Top Assembly:

Use Setting Diagram to join Blocks A and B into 6 rows. Be sure to refer to the directional arrows for correct placement of Block B. Refer to Whole Quilt Diagram and join rows.

Setting Diagram

Quilting:

For Block A, outline-quilt ¼″ from seams of the rectangle and two squares. Outline-quilt ¼″ from seams of all triangles pieced in the center and along the border. Quilt a straight line from the points of the triangles as shown. An X is formed by quilting lines from corner to corner in the two remaining squares of Block A. For Block B, quilt a set of parallel lines 1″ apart and 1″ from the base of the triangles. Outline-quilt ¼″ from seams of all triangles. Refer to Quilting Diagram before marking fabric.

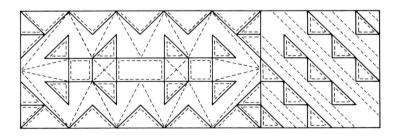

Finished Edges:

Bind raw edges with maroon fabric.

66

Lady of the Lotus

In Eastern thought the lotus blossom appears as a symbol of purity, truth, and rebirth. This particular quilt is a wish for growth, for knowledge. Let me be always as open to life's offerings as the lotus blossom is open to the sun.

As you can see, this is a challenge quilt. However, even if you've never done any strip piecing but are quite comfy with complex patchwork, you can handle this one just fine. I suggest getting engrossed in the instructions and staying right with it—no stopping in the middle to eat chocolates and watch TV! Take your breaks after each section of strip piecing has been constructed and cut out. And when you finish, don't be one bit bashful about bragging a little.

Skill Level:
    Patchwork—Advanced
    Quilting—Advanced
Finished Size: 90″ x 90″
Number of Blocks and
Finished Block Size:
    2 Block A—21¼″ x 30″ x 15″ each
    2 Block B—21¼″ x 30″ x 15″ each

2 Block C—21¼″ x 30″ x 15″ each
4 Block D—Multi-sided
2 Block E—Multi-sided
2 Block F—15″ x 42″ each
4 Block G—Multi-sided
4 Block H—34″ x 24″ x 24″ each
2 Block I—12″ x 24″ each

68

Materials:

COLOR OF FABRIC	YARDS REQUIRED	TEMPLATE REQUIRED	NUMBER TO CUT	A	B	C	D	E	F	G	H	I
Gray	⅝	23	8	—	—	—	1	2	—	—	—	—
		34	8	—	—	—	1	2	—	—	—	—
		50	2	—	1	—	—	—	—	—	—	—
Lt. Blue	1⅛	1	4	—	—	—	1	—	—	—	—	—
		28 extend to 17″	4	—	—	—	1	—	—	—	—	—
		30 extend to 21¼″	4	—	—	—	—	—	—	—	1	—
		32	4	—	—	—	—	—	—	—	1	—
		46	4	—	—	—	—	—	—	—	1	—
Aqua	1⅜	1	4	—	—	—	1	—	—	—	—	—
		28 extend to 12¾″	4	—	—	—	1	—	—	—	—	—
		30 extend to 21¼″	4	—	—	—	—	—	—	—	1	—
		39	2	—	1	—	—	—	—	—	—	—
Dk. Aqua	1	6	2	—	1	—	—	—	—	—	—	—
		46	4	—	2	—	—	—	—	—	—	—
Lt. Turq.	1½	1	4	—	—	—	1	—	—	—	—	—
		10 extend to 18″	2	—	1	—	—	—	—	—	—	—
		11 extend to 30″	2	1	—	—	—	—	—	—	—	—
		28 extend to 21¼″	4	—	—	—	1	—	—	—	—	—
		30 extend to 8½″	4	—	—	—	—	—	—	—	1	—
		30 extend to 21¼″	4	—	—	—	—	—	—	—	1	—
		46	8	—	2	—	—	—	—	—	1	—
Dk. Turq.	⅝	11 extend to 30″	2	1	—	—	—	—	—	—	—	—
Navy	⅞	1	2	—	—	—	—	—	—	—	—	1
		10 extend to 24″	2	—	1	—	—	—	—	—	—	—
		46	4	—	2	—	—	—	—	—	—	—
Rust	1¼	16	4	—	—	—	—	—	2	—	—	—
		23	20	—	—	—	—	—	6	1	—	2
		28 extend to 12¾″	4	—	—	—	—	—	—	1	—	—
		46	20	—	—	—	—	—	—	4	1	—
		49	16	—	—	—	—	2	6	—	—	—
Brown	¾	11 extend to 9″	4	—	—	—	—	—	—	—	—	2
		11 extend to 30″	2	—	—	1	—	—	—	—	—	—
		34	4	—	—	—	—	—	—	—	—	2
		46	12	—	—	—	—	—	—	3	—	—
Lt. Brown	½	11 extend to 9″	4	—	—	—	—	—	—	—	—	2
		11 extend to 30″	2	—	—	1	—	—	—	—	—	—
Yellow	½	32	8	—	—	—	1	2	—	—	—	—
		50	2	—	—	—	—	1	—	—	—	—

COLOR OF FABRIC	YARDS REQUIRED	TEMPLATE REQUIRED	NUMBER TO CUT	NUMBER USED PER BLOCK								
				A	B	C	D	E	F	G	H	I
Lt. Rust	¼	50	6	—	—	—	—	—	3	—	—	—
Orange	⅜	34	16	—	—	—	—	2	6	—	—	—
White	3½	6	2	—	—	—	—	—	—	—	—	1
		16	12	—	—	—	—	2	2	1	—	—
		23	20	—	—	—	—	—	6	2	—	—
		24	4	—	—	—	—	—	2	—	—	—
		46	24	—	—	—	—	—	—	5	—	2
		49	12	—	—	—	—	2	—	—	—	4
		50	24	6	—	6	—	—	—	—	—	—
		59	4	—	—	—	—	—	2	—	—	—
		61	4	—	—	—	—	—	—	1	—	—
		67	4	—	—	—	—	—	—	—	1	—
		68	4	—	—	—	—	—	—	1	—	—
		70	4	—	—	—	—	—	—	1	—	—
Binding: Lt. Blue	¾	—	—	—	—	—	—	—	—	—	—	—
Backing: White Cotton or Muslin	6	—	—	—	—	—	—	—	—	—	—	—

Strip Piecing:

Strip piecing should be done before any patchwork. Cut or tear all strips crosswise on the fabric. Press the strip-pieced fabric with all seams in one direction, if possible. Do this before drawing any shapes on the fabric. Draw on the front to keep from drawing over seams. Strips will be very bulky every 44″, where the strip lengths are sewn together. Skip past this spot when drawing shapes. The only seams on your shapes should be those where separate colors are joined.

There are 4 separate strip-piecing sections to be constructed. Join strips, use template to draw shapes, and cut pieces for block usage. Shaded areas on diagrams indicate waste and should be discarded to avoid confusion.

Strip Piece Construction:

Strip Piece #1—All strips are 4 fabric-widths or 176″ long. Join 1 gray, 1 aqua, and 1 dark aqua strip, in that order.

Place base of template 50 at the bottom edge of the dark aqua strip. (See Diagram for Strip Pieces #1 and #2.) Cut 20 for Block A. These pieces will be designated 1SP.

Strip Piece #2—All strips are 4 fabric-widths or 176″ long. Join 1 brown, 1 light brown, and 1 yellow strip in that order. Place template 50 at the bottom edge of the yellow strip. (See Diagram for Strip Pieces #1 and #2.) Cut 20 for Block C. These pieces will be designated 2SP.

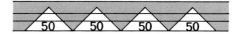

Diagram for Strip Pieces #1 and #2

Strip Piecing Chart:

COLOR OF FABRIC	YARDS REQUIRED	STRIP SIZE*	TEMPLATE REQUIRED	NUMBER OF TEMPLATES TO CUT	NUMBER USED PER BLOCK
					A B C D E F G H I
Strip Piece #1 (1SP):					
Gray	**	1⅛″ x 176″***			10 — — — — — — — —
Aqua	**	1⅛″ x 176″***	50	20	
Dark Aqua	**	1⅛″ x 176″***			
Strip Piece #2 (2SP):					
Brown	**	1⅛″ x 176″***			
Light Brown	**	1⅛″ x 176″***	50	20	— — 10 — — — — — —
Yellow	**	1⅛″ x 176″***			
Strip Piece #3 (3SP):					
Light Turquoise	**	1″ x 15″***			
Dark Turquoise	**	1⅛″ x 15″***			
Navy	**	1⅛″ x 15″***			
Dark Turquoise	**	1⅛″ x 15″***			
Light Turquoise	**	1⅛″ x 15″***	69	2	— — — — — — — — 1
Dark Aqua	**	1⅛″ x 15″***			
Aqua	**	1⅛″ x 15″***			
Gray	**	1⅛″ x 15″***			
Light Blue	**	1″ x 15″***			
Strip Piece #4 (4SP):					
Light Blue	**	1¼″ x 352″***			
Aqua	**	1⅛″ x 352″***			
Dark Aqua	**	1⅛″ x 352″***			
Light Turquoise	**	1⅛″ x 352″***	47	24	— — — — — — 6 — —
Dark Turquoise	**	1⅛″ x 352″***			
Navy	**	⅞″ x 352″***			

*—Cut 1 of each strip measurement.
**—Yardage is included in the Materials Chart.
***—Measurements are given without seam allowance.

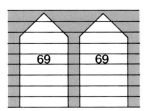

Diagram for Strip Piece #3

Strip Piece #3—All strips are 15″ long. Join strips in the following order: light turquoise, dark turquoise, navy, dark turquoise, light turquoise, dark aqua, aqua, gray, and light blue. With light blue at the bottom, place the base of template 69 at the bottom edge of the light blue strip. (See Diagram for Strip Piece #3.) Cut 2 for Block I. These pieces will be designated 3SP.

Strip Piece #4—All strips are 8 fabric-widths, or approximately 9⅞ yards, long. Join strips in the following order: light blue, aqua, dark aqua, light turquoise, dark turquoise, and navy. With navy at the bottom, place the base of template 47 at the bottom edge of the navy strip. (See Diagram for Strip Pieces #1 and #2 for layout configuration.) Cut 24 for Block G. These pieces will be designated 4SP.

Block Assembly:

This quilt contains 9 different blocks. Join pieces and sections for each block as indicated by the diagrams. *Refer to Whole Quilt Diagram for proper color placement.* Arrow on final assembly diagrams indicates top of block.

BLOCK A

Each block contains 2 sections. Join pieces and sections as indicated by the diagrams. Make 2 blocks.

Section 1—Join 1 white template 50 with strip-pieced template 50 (1SP), to form a basic unit. Make 12. Six will be used in each block. Join 6 basic units with four 1SP to form triangle as shown.

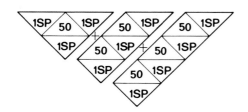

Block Diagram for Quilt Top

Block A Sections

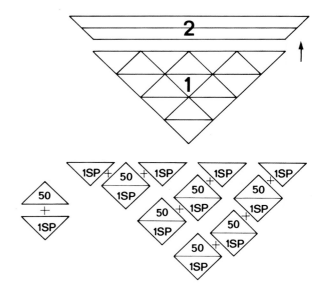

Section 2—Sew together strips of light turquoise and dark turquoise.

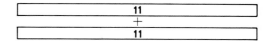

72

Final Assembly: Lay template 50 on strip piece (Section 2) and cut right and left sides as shown. Join strip piece to triangle.

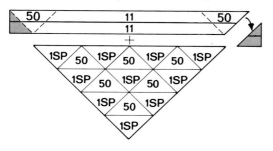

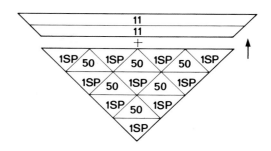

BLOCK B

Each block contains 2 sections. Join pieces and sections as indicated by the diagrams. Make 2 blocks.

Block B Sections

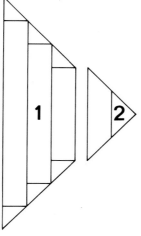

Section 1

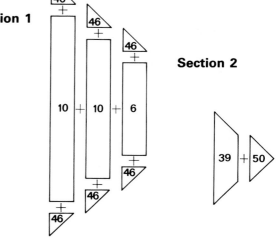

Section 2

Final Assembly

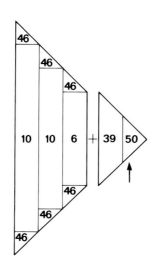

BLOCK C

Block C is pieced the same as Block A. Use template 50 of 2SP to make the basic unit. Make 2 blocks.

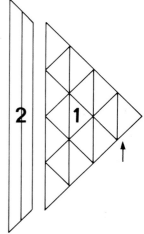

73

BLOCK D

Each block contains 3 sections. Join pieces and sections as indicated by the diagrams. There is one pivot point in the final assembly. Make 2 blocks as shown and 2 blocks the mirror image of these for a total of 4 blocks.

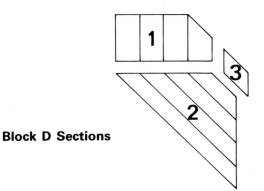

Block D Sections

Section 1

Section 2

Section 3—Template 32.

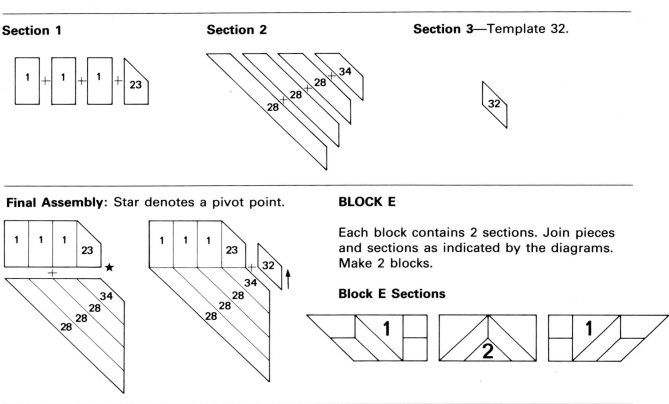

Final Assembly: Star denotes a pivot point.

BLOCK E

Each block contains 2 sections. Join pieces and sections as indicated by the diagrams. Make 2 blocks.

Block E Sections

Section 1—Star denotes a pivot point. Make 2 per block, with 1 the mirror image of the other.

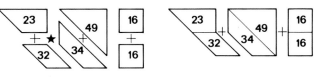

Section 2—Star denotes a pivot point.

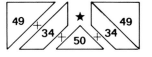

Final Assembly: Arrow indicates top of the block.

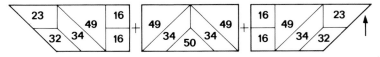

74

BLOCK F

Each block contains 5 sections. Join pieces and sections as indicated by the diagrams. Make 2 blocks.

Block F Sections

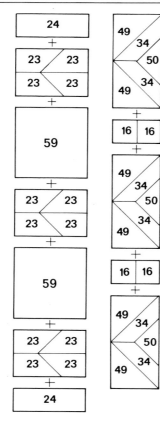

Section 1—Make 3 per block.

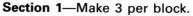

Section 2—Template 24. Need 2 per block.

Section 3—Template 59. Need 2 per block.

Section 4—Make 3 per block. Star denotes a pivot point.

Section 5—Make 2 per block.

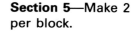

Final Assembly

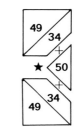
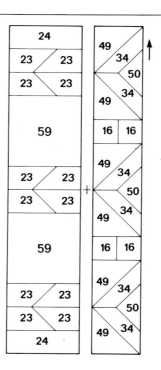

75

BLOCK G

Each block contains 3 sections. Join pieces and sections as indicated by the diagrams. Make 2 blocks as shown and 2 blocks the mirror image of these. To help you join the long bias edges of templates 61, 68, and 70, fold each piece in half to find center and align centers before sewing.

Block G Sections

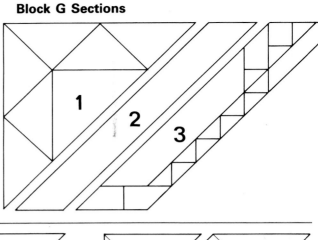

Section 1—Use template 47 of 4SP.

Section 2—Template 70.

Section 3

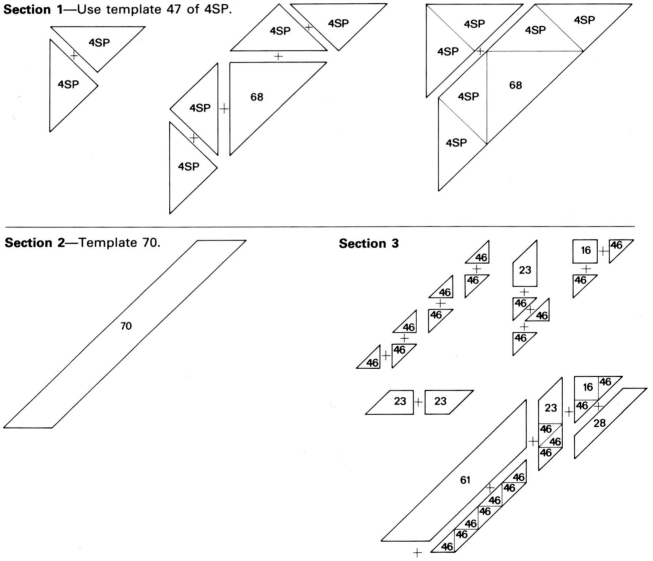

76

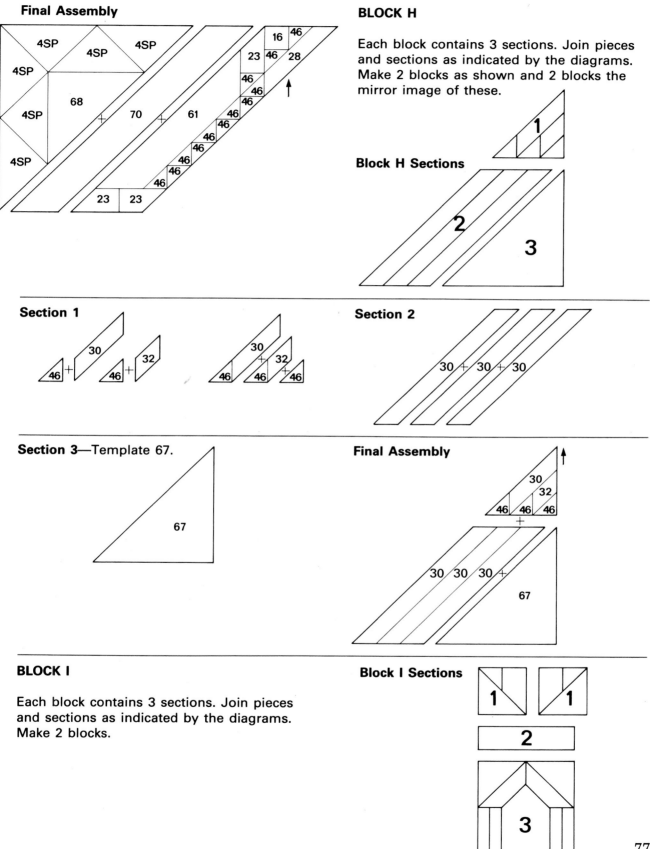

Final Assembly

BLOCK H

Each block contains 3 sections. Join pieces and sections as indicated by the diagrams. Make 2 blocks as shown and 2 blocks the mirror image of these.

Block H Sections

Section 1

Section 2

Section 3—Template 67.

Final Assembly

BLOCK I

Each block contains 3 sections. Join pieces and sections as indicated by the diagrams. Make 2 blocks.

Block I Sections

Section 1—Make 2 per block, with 1 the mirror image of the other.

Section 2—Template 6.

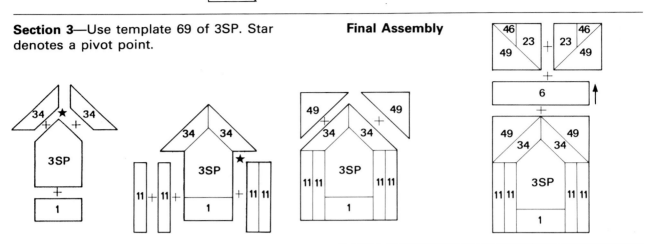

Section 3—Use template 69 of 3SP. Star denotes a pivot point.

Final Assembly

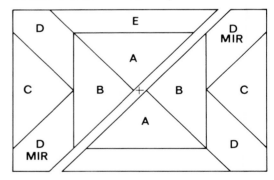

Quilt Top Assembly:

Join the Center Section first. Arrows on diagram indicate the top of each block.

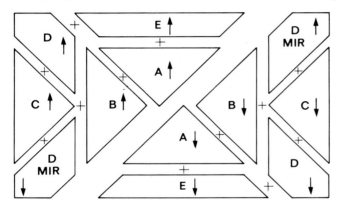

Center Section Assembly

Row Assembly—Join blocks into rows. Center Section is one large unit.

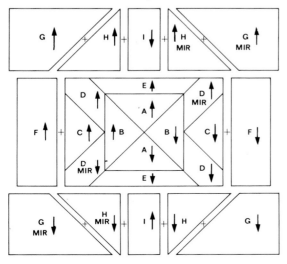

Final Assembly: Join rows.

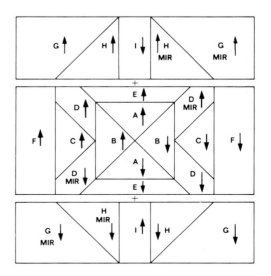

Quilting:

The quilting on *Lady of the Lotus* requires care and an even temper at the marking stage. The use of masking tape may help when marking for straight-line quilting. If using a quilting pattern other than clamshells for the white areas, choose a rather extensive one. These white areas are large, with long bias seams that cannot be skimpily stitched. Too little quilting may cause the outer edges of the quilt to sag and stretch.

To make quilting instructions as simple as possible, the quilt has been divided into quilting sections, as shown in the diagram. Some sections coincide with block seam lines, but many do not. (The interconnecting circle and fleur-de-lis quilting patterns are reprinted with permission from Shirley Thompson. They appear in her book, *The Finishing Touch*, published by Powell Publications, Edmonds, Washington, in 1980.) Quilting patterns are found in Pattern Section.

Quilting Sections

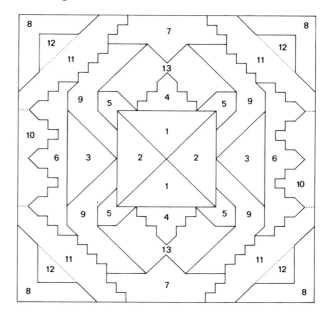

Section 1—This is the same as Block A. Parallel quilting lines on strip piecing and strip-pieced triangles are ½" apart and ¼" from seams. Parallel quilting lines on the remaining triangles are ¼" apart and ¼" from seams.

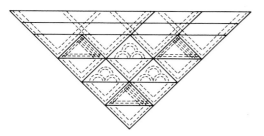

Section 2—This is the same as Block B. Parallel quilting lines are 1" apart and ¼" from block seam line.

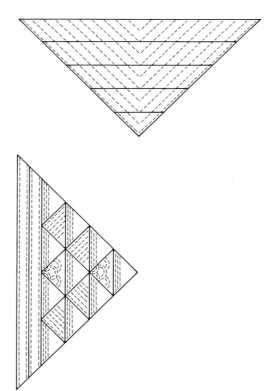

Section 3—This is the same as Block C. Narrow parallel quilting lines are all contained in the bottom strip of the strip-pieced triangles. They are ¼" apart and ¼" from the seam. Parallel quilting lines for the remaining triangles are ½" apart and ¼" from seams. Outline quilting lines are ¼" from seams.

79

Section 4—Outline-quilt ¼″ from seams. Parallel quilting lines are ½″ apart.

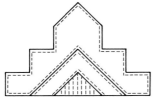

Section 5—Outline-quilt ¼″ from seams. Parallel quilting lines are ½″ apart.

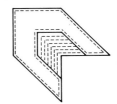

Section 6—Outline-quilt ¼″ from seams. Parallel quilting lines are ¾″ apart.

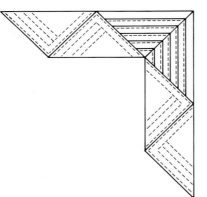

Section 7—Outline-quilt ¼″ from seams. Parallel quilting lines on the diagonal are ¾″ apart. Quilt in-the-ditch of the first 5 seams of the strip-pieced section (template 69 of Block I). Use the top segment of fleur-de-lis quilting pattern for corner triangles.

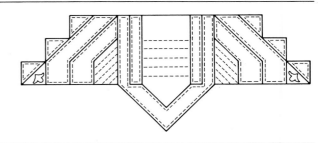

Section 8—Outline-quilt ¼″ from seams. Parallel quilting lines are 1″ apart.

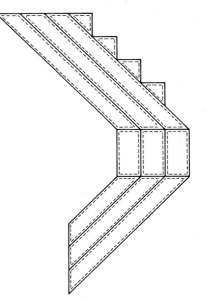

Section 9—Outline-quilt ¼″ from all seams.

80

Section 10—Use the interconnecting circle quilting pattern and quilt as shown.

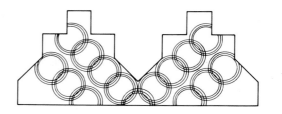

Section 11—Use fleur-de-lis quilting pattern. Begin by drawing the top segment of the pattern centered in the 4 triangles. The widest part of this segment should be ¼" from the side seams of the triangle.

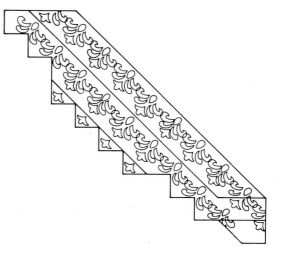

For the second row, the fleur-de-lis is drawn ¼" from the seam below it. Each pattern is centered directly below the top segment. The designs will overlap each other as shown on the diagram. A partial pattern is drawn and centered under each corner. There should be a total of 4 complete patterns and 5 incomplete patterns on the second row. (Extending a quilting line from the bottom tip of the top segment to the top of the second row is the quilter's option. It requires quilting over a seam, which is not the preference of some quilters.)

For the third row, the fleur-de-lis is also drawn ¼" from the seam below it and centered directly below the pattern above it. Continue placing the pattern as you did on the second row. There should be a total of 8 complete patterns and 2 incomplete patterns for this row.

Section 12 and Section 13—Quilt a clamshell pattern in these sections. (The double clamshell pattern I used is from The Great American Coverup, Dallas, Texas.)

Section 12

Section 13

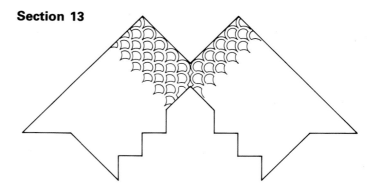

Finished Edges:
Bind raw edges with light blue fabric.

Irish Gentleman

Whatever his nationality, the gentleman is not a fussy, frilly type. The true gentleman, though, has room in his heart for tenderness, compassion, for love—hence, the inclusion of a bit of pink in this quilt. It counter-balances the stark lines of the rest of the design, like the qualities that make a man a gentleman.

Skill Level:
   Patchwork—Intermediate (elongated triangles)
   Quilting—Intermediate (large amount of straight-line quilting)
Finished Size: 87" x 87"
Number of Blocks and Finished Block Size:
   9 Blocks—21" x 21" each

Materials:

COLOR OF FABRIC	YARDS REQUIRED	TEMPLATE REQUIRED	NUMBER TO CUT	NUMBER USED PER BLOCK
Green	3	16	36	4
		40	36	4
		46	36	4
Pink	1	16	27	3
		46	36	4
White	5½	1	36	4
		5	18	2
		16	36	4
		40	36	4
		49	36	4
Joining Strips: Green	*	16	24	—
Pink	*	16	16	—
White	*	24	48	—
Border: Green	*	16	8	—
		27	16	—
		40	16	—
		1½" x 81"**	4	—
Pink	*	16	4	—
White	*	27	24	—
		1½" x 81"**	4	—
Binding: Green	¾	—	—	—
Backing: Green	6	—	—	—

*—Yardage is included in above measurement.
**—Measurements are given without seam allowance.

Block Assembly:

Each block contains 3 sections. Join pieces and sections as indicated by the diagrams. Make 9 blocks.

Block Sections

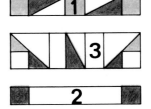

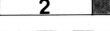

Section 1

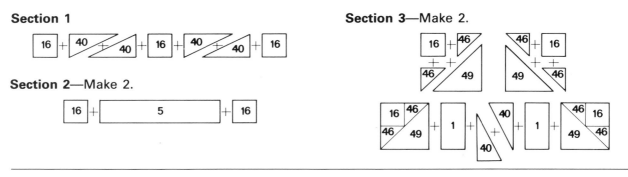

Section 3—Make 2.

Section 2—Make 2.

Final Assembly: Join sections, rotating one Section 3, as shown.

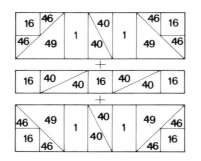

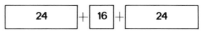

Joining Strip Assembly:

Horizontal Joining Strips—Make 24. Set aside 12 for use in constructing vertical joining strips.

Vertical Joining Strips—Alternate 3 horizontal joining strips with 4 squares (template 16) and join. Make 4 strips (shown horizontally because of space restrictions).

Border Assembly:

First Border—Make 4. Add a template-16 square to each side of 2 borders. Refer to Whole Quilt Diagram for color placement.

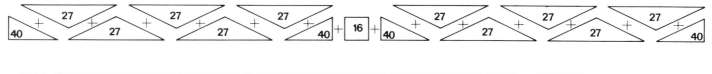

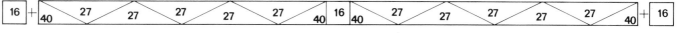

Second Border—Join 1½″ border strips lengthwise. Make 4. Add a template-16 square to each end of 2 borders. Refer to Whole Quilt Diagram for color placement.

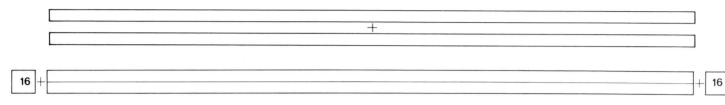

Quilt Top Assembly:

Alternate 3 blocks with 4 horizontal joining strips and join. Make 3 vertical rows. Alternate 3 vertical rows with 4 vertical joining strips and join. Join shorter first border to top and bottom and longer first border to sides of quilt. Join shorter second border to top and bottom and longer second border to sides of quilt. (See Whole Quilt Diagram for proper border placement.)

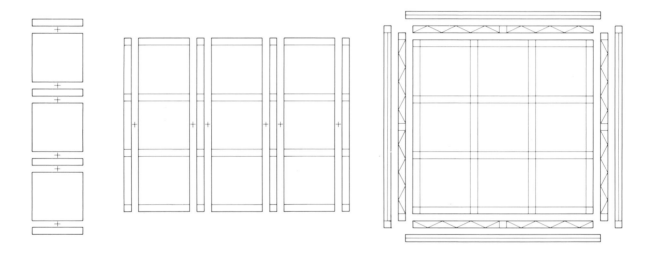

Quilting:

Outline quilting is ¼″ from seams. Parallel quilting lines in the white squares of the block are ⅛″ apart and ¼″ from seams. Parallel quilting lines in the white rectangles of the block and joining strips are ⅝″ apart and ¼″ from seams. Parallel quilting lines for the center of the block are 1″ apart and ¼″ from seams.

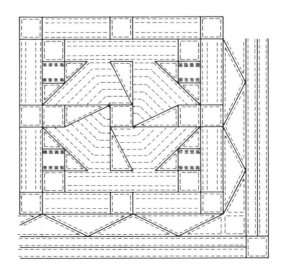

Finished Edges:

Bind raw edges with green fabric.

It's Obvious

What's obvious about this quilt may be different for each viewer. It was initially intended as a "play" quilt—that is, playing with the number 9. The piecework uses only squares and triangles, so it is the perfect quilt for using all those little snatches of fabric in your sewing basket.

Skill Level:
    Patchwork—Beginner
    Quilting—Beginner
Finished Size: 90″ x 96″
Number of Blocks and
Finished Block Size:
    20 Blocks—18″ x 24″ each

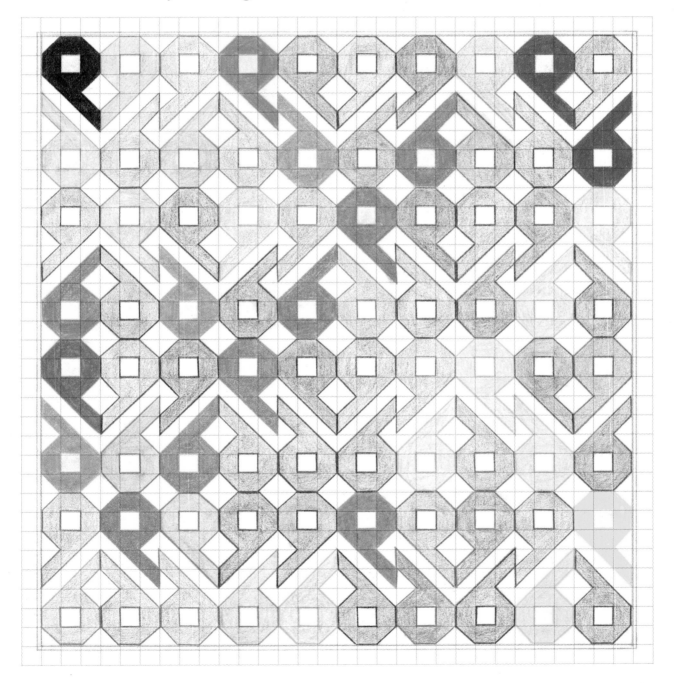

Materials:

COLOR OF FABRIC	YARDS REQUIRED	TEMPLATE REQUIRED	NUMBER TO CUT	NUMBER USED PER BLOCK
Scrap	¼ each of 40 different fabrics	16 46	8* 14*	16 28
White	4¼	16 46	80 560	4 28
Binding: White	¾	—	—	—
Backing: White Cotton or Muslin	6¼	—	—	—

*—Number to cut per fabric.

Block Assembly:

Each block contains 3 sections. Join pieces and sections for each block as indicated by the diagrams. Randomly use scrap fabric pieces for your number design. Make 20 blocks.

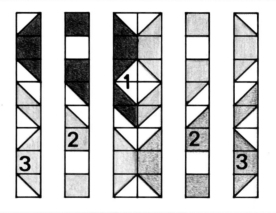

Block Sections

Section 1—Each pieced column is a mirror image of the other. Join columns.

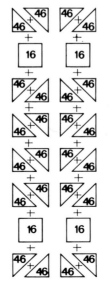
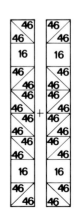

Section 2—Each pieced column is a mirror image of the other.

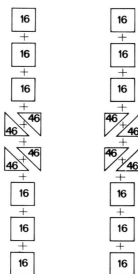

Section 3—Each pieced column is a mirror image of the other.

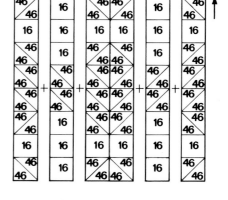

Final Assembly: Join columns in the following sectional order: 3-2-1-2-3. Set blocks in 4 rows of 5 blocks each, turning every other block upside down. (See Setting Diagram and Whole Quilt Diagram.) Arrow indicates top of block.

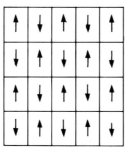

Setting Diagram

Quilting:
Outline-quilt ¼″ from seams.

Finished Edges:
Bind raw edges with white fabric.

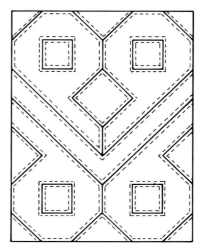

91

Crescendo

Crescendo is a dynamic marking in music. It means "to get louder." When the beginning piano student encounters this marking, it's time to stop just "pecking around" and really begin to play music. My piano teacher, bless her soul, persevered and transformed me from a piano student into a musician. "Put some feeling into it," she'd squawk and rap on my knuckles with her two-foot-long pencil with a little boxing glove on the end. The grand piano was huge; her pencil was huge; and *she* was huge, though she could cross the room in a flash with pencil waving, executing her own crescendo if I played a wrong note. So, it seems fitting that the visual crescendo in this quilt should also be huge.

Skill Level:
　Patchwork—Advanced
　Quilting—Intermediate
Finished Size: 90″ x 90″
**Number of Blocks and
Finished Block Size:**
　10 Blocks—30″ x 15″ each
**Number of Side Units and
Finished Side Unit Size:**
　2 Units—60″ x 30″ each

Materials:

COLOR OF FABRIC	YARDS REQUIRED	TEMPLATE REQUIRED	NUMBER TO CUT	NUMBER USED PER BLOCK	NUMBER USED PER SIDE UNIT
Maroon	3½	1	24	2	2
		12	8	—	4
		22 extend to 9″	10	1	—
		22F* extend to 9″	10	1	—
		32	10	1	—
		32F*	10	1	—
		34	20	2	—
		37	4	—	2
		43	4	—	2
		43F*	4	—	2
		46	28	2	4
		50	4	—	2
		54 extend to 21¼″	2	—	1
		54F* extend to 21¼″	2	—	1
Blue Print	2¾	1	4	—	2
		12	8	—	4
		23	20	2	—
		23F*	20	2	—
		29 extend to 23¼″	2	—	1
		29F* extend to 23¼″	2	—	1
		32	10	1	—
		32F*	10	1	—
		36	4	—	2
		43	2	—	1
		43F*	2	—	1
		46	28	2	4
		49	4	—	2
		50	2	—	1
White	5½	1	22	2	1
		10 extend to 18″	10	1	—
		12	4	—	2
		23	20	2	—
		32	40	4	—
		43	4	—	2
		46	84	8	2
		48	4	—	2
		49	28	2	4
		50	14	1	2
		54 extend to 21¼″	4	—	2
Binding: Blue Print	¾	—	—	—	—
Backing: White Cotton or Muslin	6	—	—	—	—

*—Flip or turn over template if fabric is one-sided.

Block Assembly:

Join pieces and sections for each block as indicated by the diagrams. Make 10 blocks.

Block Sections

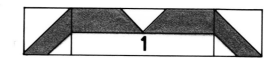

Section 1

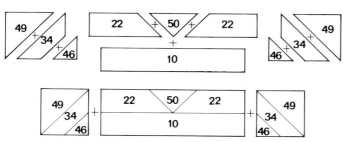

Section 2

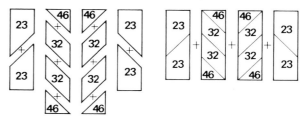

Section 3—For Section 3, there will be 2 separate blocks when finished. One will be the mirror image of the other.

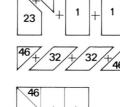

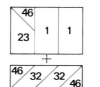

Final Assembly

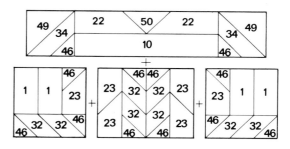

Side Unit:

Make 2 side units. Join pieces and sections as indicated by diagrams.

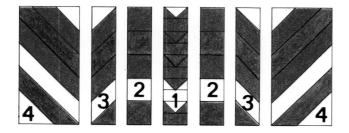

Section 1—Make 5 small blocks. Join as shown.

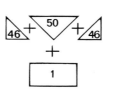

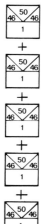

95

Section 2—Make 2.

Section 3—One is the mirror image of the other. Make 2.

Section 4—One is the mirror image of the other. Make 2.

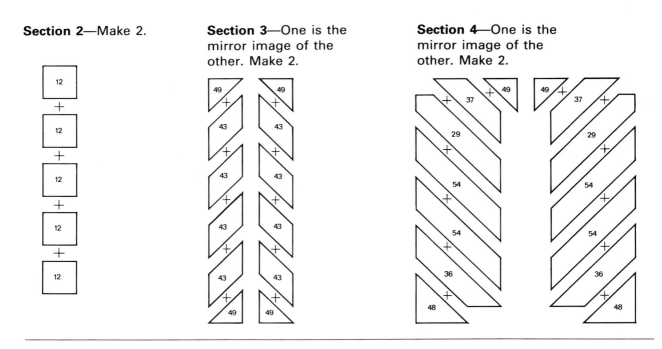

Final Assembly: Starred side indicates outside edge. (See Whole Quilt Diagram.)

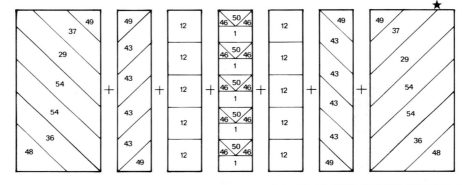

Quilt Top Assembly:

Quilting:

Block—Outline-quilt ¼″ from seams as indicated. Parallel quilting lines for white corner triangles at the top of the block are ¾″ apart and ¼″ from seam. Parallel quilting lines for white triangle at center and top of the block are ½″ apart and ¼″ from seam. Parallel quilting lines for white corner triangles at the bottom of the block are ½″ apart and ¼″ from seam. Parallel quilting lines for the 2 template-46 white triangles in the middle of the block are ½″ apart and ¼″ from seam. Parallel quilting lines in white area that forms a modified M are ½″ apart and ¼″ from seams. Remainder of parallel quilting lines are 1″ from the outline quilting.

Side Unit—Outline-quilt ¼″ from seams as indicated. The star indicates outside edge of unit. Parallel quilting lines for the triangle in the center of outside edge are ½″ apart and ¼″ from seams. Parallel quilting lines for the 2 remaining large white triangles on the outside edge are ¾″ apart and ¼″ from seams. Because of the angle interplay in the mid-section of this unit, parallel quilting lines will automatically be farther apart in this area, as noted by the dotted lines on the diagram. For the first band of red from the outside edge, parallel quilting lines are ¾″ apart and ¼″ from seams and become 1″ apart where dotted lines are shown. For the first band of blue from the outside edge, parallel quilting lines are 1″ apart and ¼″ from seams and become 1¼″ apart where dotted lines are shown. The next band of red is quilted the same as the previous red band. For the band of white, parallel quilting lines are ¾″ apart and ¼″ from seams and become 1″ apart where dotted lines are shown. For the next band of blue, parallel quilting lines are 1″ apart and ¼″ from seams. Parallel quilting lines for the corner white triangles are ¾″ apart and ¼″ from seams.

Finished Edges:

Bind raw edges with blue print fabric.

97

Jam Session

Ever wonder what musicians mean when they say they're "gonna go jam with some friends"? Jamming is to musicians what brainstorming is to think tanks—a spontaneous outpouring of creativity, tossing an idea around to see what happens, a journey without a planned destination. Everybody plays their best licks, back and forth, and the resulting spur-of-the-moment composition is probably forever lost to posterity because the tape wasn't running.

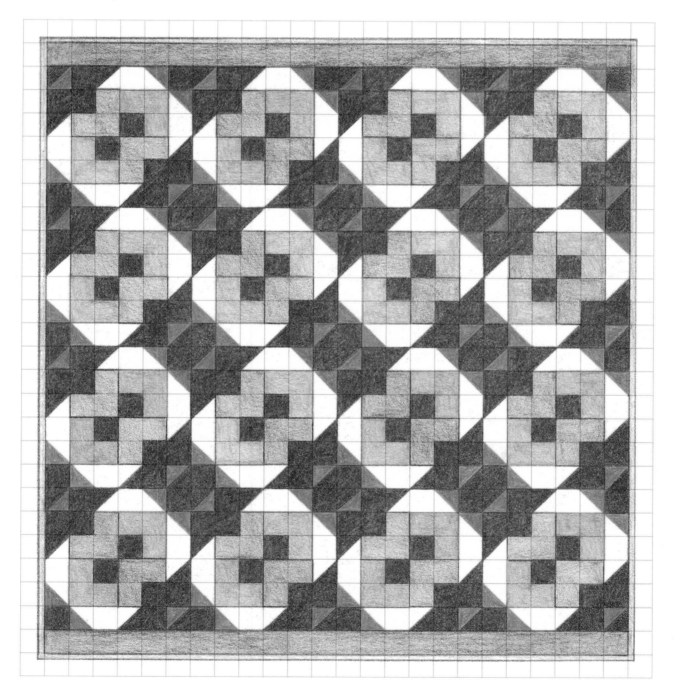

Sometimes a band will jam in rehearsal to keep from going stale—ideas appear in a jam that may later occur in performance. Sometimes a band will jam to loosen up before a big concert.

But jamming isn't reserved for rehearsal. It can happen on stage, too. And soon the band is jamming for the sheer joy of it, excited with playing things they've never played before and hearing things they've never heard before.

This pattern turned out to be quite a jam itself. I've learned so much from jamming with musicians who are better than me—this quilt is no exception. When I made the quilt, I used a piecing arrangement that split the blocks into quarters. This made it very simple to piece, but it left a rather unsatisfactory dispersion of seams and required too many patches.

The design first appeared in print in June 1979, in *Quilter's Newsletter Magazine*. The editor, Bonnie Leman, took my original instructions and made some much-needed improvements in them. Her ideas about piecing arrangement are reprinted here with permission. Mary Leman Austin played with the design and suggested other possibilities. Bonnie and Mary—thank you for sitting in and adding some great licks to this *Jam Session*.

Skill Level:
    Patchwork—Intermediate (pivot points)
    Quilting—Beginner
Finished Size: 72″ x 78″
Number of Blocks and
Finished Block Size:
    16 Blocks—18″ x 18″ each

Materials:

COLOR OF FABRIC	YARDS REQUIRED	TEMPLATE REQUIRED	NUMBER TO CUT	NUMBER USED PER BLOCK
Brown	2½	16	96	6
		23	32	2
		23F*	32	2
		46	32	2
Gingham**	1¾	23	32	2
		23F*	32	2
Print	1¼	23	32	2
		23F*	32	2
Orange	¾	46	96	6
Muslin	1¾	33	64	4
Border: Gingham	***	3″ x 36″****	4	—
Binding: Gingham	½	—	—	—
Backing: White Cotton or Muslin	4½	—	—	—

    *—Flip or turn over template if fabric is one-sided.
    **—See Dominoes Quilt for notation regarding the use of gingham.
    ***—Yardage is included in the above measurement.
    ****—Measurement is given without seam allowance.

Block Assembly:

Each block contains 3 sections. Join pieces and sections as indicated by the diagrams. Make 16 blocks.

Block Sections

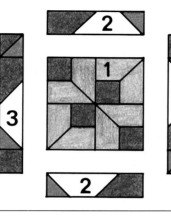

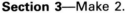

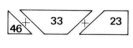

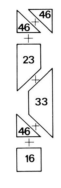

Section 1—Make all of the basic units that require pivot points first. (See section on Pivot Points in the General Instructions.)

Basic Unit

Each block contains 4 basic units. Join basic units into 2 columns, rotating them as shown. Join columns.

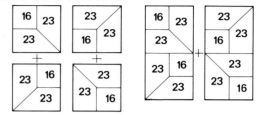

Section 2—Make 2.

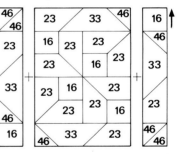

Section 3—Make 2.

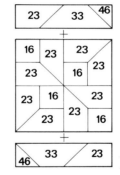

Final Assembly: Join Section 2s to top and bottom of Section 1, rotating one as shown. Join Section 3s to the sides, rotating one as shown. Arrow indicates top of block.

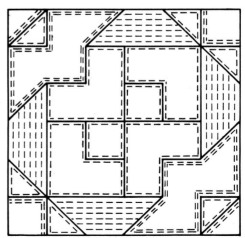

Border Assembly:

Sew two 36″ strips together at ends to form one 72″ strip. Make two 72″ strips.

Quilt Top Assembly:

Join blocks in 4 rows of 4 blocks each, making sure that all blocks are right side up. (See Whole Quilt Diagram.) Join rows and add border strips to the top and bottom of quilt.

Quilting:

Outline quilting is ¼″ from seams. Parallel quilting lines contained within the muslin trapezoids are ½″ apart and ¼″ from seams. The remaining parallel quilting lines are ¼″ apart and ¼″ from seams.

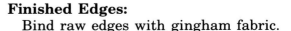

Finished Edges:

Bind raw edges with gingham fabric.

Gnothi Seauton

Gnothi Seauton, "know thyself," is an inscription on the ancient temple of Apollo at Delphi. For most of recorded history, people have followed this maxim with varying degrees of success.

And what will historians write of our era? Will they write that the late 20th century was a time of human enlightenment? Will they write that we spent our time developing technology, or that we also explored the realms of the human heart and spirit? What history says about the human race can only be determined by the individual effort of each of us.

These directions are for beginners. Intermediate and advanced quilters may wish to piece blocks with pivot points by using a square in the center, rather than two triangles. (See photograph and Quilting Diagram.) If so, cut 36 of template 16, instead of 72 of template 46.

Setting diagrams are given for three variations. Have fun exploring them!

Materials:

COLOR OF FABRIC	YARDS REQUIRED	TEMPLATE REQUIRED	NUMBER TO CUT	NUMBER USED PER BLOCK
Rust	2½	22F* extend to 9"	72	2
		23	72	2
Pumpkin	2½	22 extend to 9"	72	2
		23F*	72	2
Peach	1¾	4	144	4
		16	72	2
White	2	4	72	2
		25	72	2
		46	72	2
Binding: Rust	¾	—	—	—
Backing: White Cotton or Muslin	6	—	—	—

*—Flip or turn over template if fabric is one-sided.

Skill Level:
    Patchwork—Beginner
    Quilting—Beginner
Finished Size: 90″ x 90″
**Number of Blocks and
Finished Block Size:**
    36 Blocks—15″ x 15″ each

Block Assembly:
   Each block contains 2 identical sections,
one of which is rotated before joining.
Make 36 blocks.

Block Sections

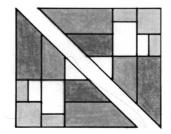

103

Section Assembly—Make 2.

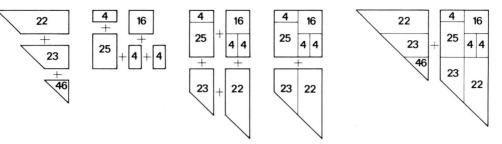

Final Assembly: Rotate one section and join to the other to complete block. (Be gentle because this seam is all bias!) Arrow indicates top of the block.

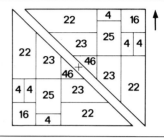

Quilt Top Assembly:

Choose one of three setting arrangements illustrated by the Whole Quilt Diagrams. Use Setting Diagrams for proper block placement. Directional arrows indicate top of the blocks.

Setting #1—This is the quilt shown in the photograph. Join blocks into 6 rows of 6 blocks each; or make 4 quadrants with 9 blocks each, and then join the 4 quadrants.

Setting Diagram

Setting #2—Join blocks into 6 rows of 6 blocks each; or make 2 halves by using 18 blocks, and then join the halves with a vertical seam up the middle.

Setting Diagram

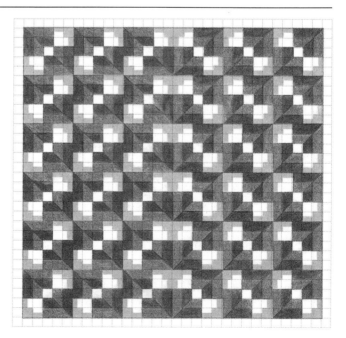

104

Setting #3—Join blocks in groups of 4. Make 9 of these units. Join units into 3 rows of 3 units each.

Setting #3 Variation—This is achieved by substituting a dark color for the white fabric.

Setting Diagram

Quilting:

Outline-quilt ¼″ from seams as shown. Straight-line-quilt along diagonal lines.

Finished Edges:

Bind raw edges with rust fabric.

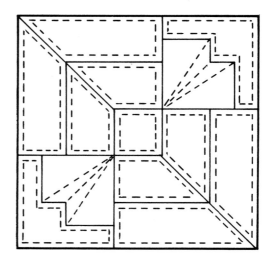

Basket Weaving

As anyone who's ever tried it knows, basket weaving is not as simple as the jokes make it out to be. In quilt form, however, it is easy enough for the beginner. The quilt's complex geometric display is the result of a repeating block, set in different directions.

Skill Level:
    Patchwork—Beginner
    Quilting—Beginner
Finished Size: 90″ x 90″
Number of Blocks and
Finished Block Size:
    36 Blocks—15″ x 15″ each

Materials:

COLOR OF FABRIC	YARDS REQUIRED	TEMPLATE REQUIRED	NUMBER TO CUT	NUMBER USED PER BLOCK
Blue	4½	23	36	1
		23F*	36	1
		28 extend to 12¾"	36	1
		28 extend to 21¼"	36	1
		34	36	1
		46	36	1
White	1¾	34	36	1
		46	144	4
Brown	3½	1	36	1
		22 extend to 9"	36	1
		28 extend to 17"	36	1
		34	36	1
Binding: Blue	¾	—	—	—
Backing: White Cotton or Muslin	6	—	—	—

*—Flip or turn over template if fabric is one-sided.

Block Assembly:

Each block contains 2 sections. Join pieces and sections as indicated by the diagrams. Make 36 blocks.

Block Sections

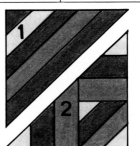

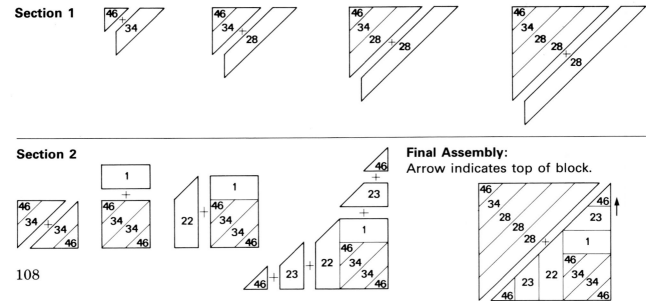

Section 1

Section 2

Final Assembly:
Arrow indicates top of block.

108

Quilt Top Assembly:

Unit Assembly—Join 2 blocks to form a unit as shown.

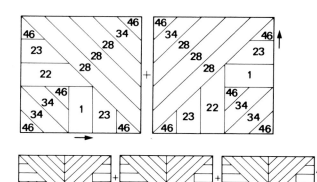

Row Assembly—Join 3 units to form a row. Make 6 rows. Arrow indicates top of the row.

Final Assembly—Join rows in 2 sets of 3 rows. Rotate one set to face the other and join. (See Whole Quilt Diagram.)

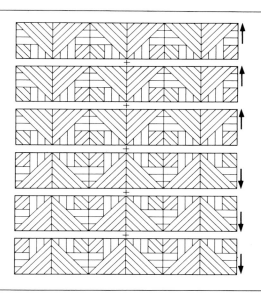

Quilting:

Outline-quilt ¼″ from seams as shown. Make a quilting template of the arch-shaped pattern in these instructions. Using this template, mark quilting lines on triangle formed where units are joined (2 of template 46). Refer to Quilting Diagram before marking fabric.

Finished Edges:

Bind raw edges with blue fabric.

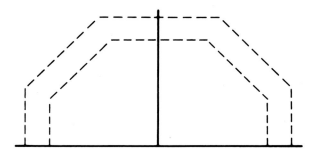

Basket Weaving Variation

Skill Level:
  Patchwork—Beginner
  Quilting—Beginner
Finished Size: 90″ x 90″

Number of Blocks and Finished Block Size:
  20 Block A—15″ x 15″ each
  4 Block B—30″ x 30″ each

Materials:

COLOR OF FABRIC	YARDS REQUIRED	TEMPLATE REQUIRED	NUMBER TO CUT	NUMBER USED PER	
				BLOCK A	BLOCK B
Blue	4¼	6	12	—	3
		23	24	1	1
		23F*	24	1	1
		24	12	—	3
		28 extend to 12¾"	24	1	1
		28 extend to 21¼"	24	1	1
		34	36	1	4
		46	24	1	1
Gold	2¼	5	12	—	3
		6	12	—	3
		34	24	1	1
		46	120	4	10
Orange	3	1	36	1	4
		22 extend to 9"	24	1	1
		24	12	—	3
		28 extend to 17"	24	1	1
		34	36	1	4
Binding: Blue	¾	—	—	—	—
Backing: White Cotton or Muslin	6	—	—	—	—

*—Flip or turn over template if fabric is one-sided.

Block Assembly:

Assemble Blocks A and B as directed.

Block A

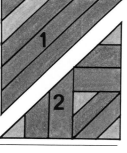

This is the same block configuration as seen in the block for *Basket Weaving.* Refer to those diagrams for piecing instructions. Make 20 blocks.

Block B

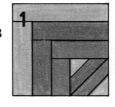
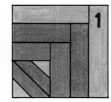
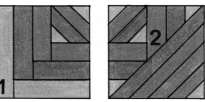

Block B contains 2 different sections. Join pieces and sections as indicated by diagrams. Make 4 blocks.

Section 1—Make 12. Arrow indicates top of section.

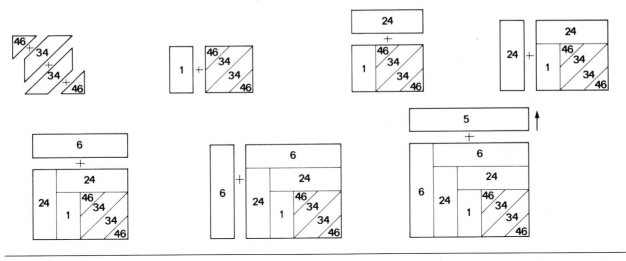

Section 2—Make 4. This is the same block configuration as seen in the block for *Basket Weaving.* Refer to those diagrams for piecing instructions.

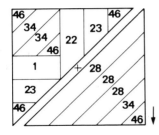

Final Assembly: Join three of Section 1 with one of Section 2, rotating sections as shown.

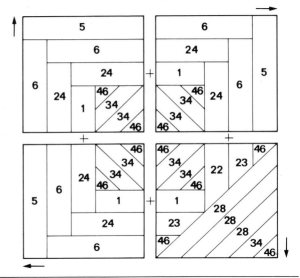

Quilt Top Assembly:

Strip Assembly

Unit Assembly—Join 2 of Block A to form a unit. Make 10 units.

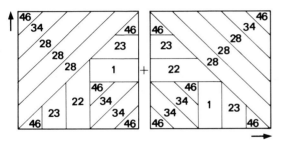

Top and Bottom Strips—Join 2 units as shown. Make 2.

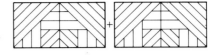

Side Strips—Join 3 units as shown. Make 2.

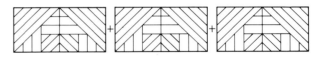

Center Section

Join 4 of Block B, rotating blocks as shown.

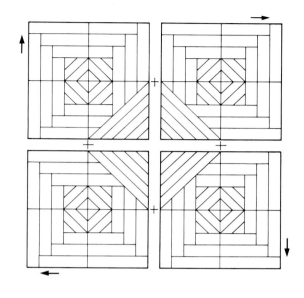

Final Assembly:

Arrange strips as shown in diagram for assembly to center section. Join top and bottom strips first and then side strips.

Quilting:

Outline-quilt ¼" from seams as shown for entire quilt top.

For center section, make a quilting template of the arch-shaped pattern found in the instructions for *Basket Weaving*. Use this template twice to make an octagon shape for quilting in the center diamond of Block B. There are 4 more of these diamonds in the center section.

For strips, use arch-shaped quilting template to mark quilting lines for the center triangle formed where two of Block A are joined to form a unit. Refer to quilting diagram before marking fabric.

Finished Edges:

Bind raw edges with blue fabric.

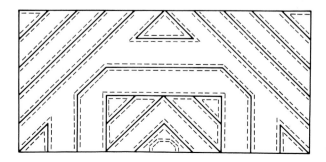

Home Cookin'

Everybody knows what home cookin' is, but some of us don't get it as often as we'd like. We're too busy, so we skip meals; we're too rushed, and prepared foods are quicker; we're never home at mealtime, so we eat out; we live alone, and cooking is too much trouble. Worst of all, cooking gets relegated to the level of a chore. Home cookin' is not just what we eat, but the underlying sense of family, which is probably what we crave. It is our state of mind when we eat that best defines home cookin'. This quilt is only a small reminder of the warm delightful feelings that accompanied suppers when I was a child—a reminder not to lose sight of the importance of "family."

Skill Level:
  Patchwork—Beginner
  Quilting—Beginner
Finished Size: 82" x 82"
**Number of Blocks and
Finished Block Size:**
  9 Blocks—24" x 24" each

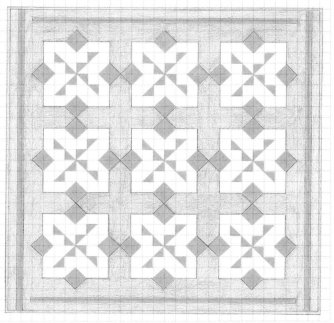

Materials:

COLOR OF FABRIC	YARDS REQUIRED	TEMPLATE REQUIRED	NUMBER TO CUT	NUMBER USED PER BLOCK
Rose	2¼	46	72	8
		50	72	8
White	3	22 extend to 9″	72	8
		23	36	4
		46	36	4
Print	2¾	22 extend to 9″	18	2
		22F* extend to 9″	18	2
		22 extend to 12″	18	2
		22F* extend to 12″	18	2
Border Strips: Rose	**	1″ x 72″***	2	—
		1″ x 82″***	2	—
Print	**	2″ x 72″***	4	—
		2″ x 82″***	4	—
Binding: Print	¾	—	—	—
Backing: White Cotton or Muslin	5½	—	—	—

*—Flip or turn over template if fabric is one-sided.
**—Yardage is included in above measurement.
***—Measurements are given without seam allowance.

Block Assembly:

Each block contains 3 sections. Join pieces and sections as indicated by the diagrams. Make 9 blocks.

Block Sections

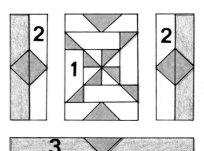

Section 1

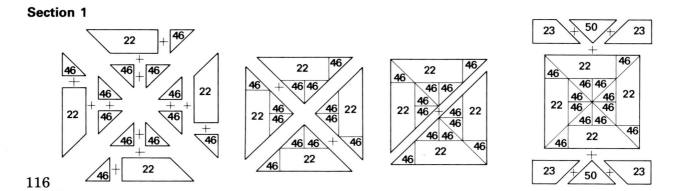

116

Section 2—Make 2.

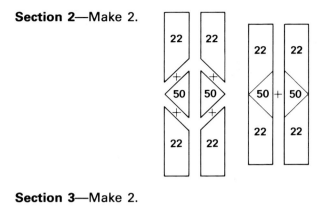

Section 3—Make 2.

Final Assembly: Rotate one Section 2 and one Section 3 before joining to Section 1 as shown. Join blocks into 3 rows of 3 blocks each. (See Whole Quilt Diagram.)

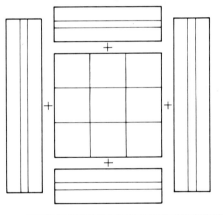

Border Strip Assembly:

Alternate two 72″ strips of printed fabric with one rose strip and join lengthwise. Make 2.

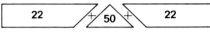

Alternate two 82″ strips of printed fabric with one rose strip and join lengthwise. Make 2.

Finished width for each strip is 5″.

Quilt Top Assembly:

Join 72″ border strips to top and bottom. Join an 82″ border strip to each side. (See Whole Quilt Diagram.)

Quilting:

Outline-quilt ¼″ from seams as shown. Parallel quilting lines are ½″ apart and ¼″ from seams.

Finished Edges:

Bind raw edges with printed fabric.

Tori's Star

Tori's Star is a celebration of young womanhood. Because there are no quilters in Tori's family, she and her mother engaged me to design a quilt that would help in the process of transforming a child's room into a teenager's room. "Let's get rid of the bunnies and kitties," Tori said. So we did. Tori supplied ideas and inspirations at every stage of this project. She wanted a quilt that would suit her now, still be appealing when she is 20, and become a family treasure later. The scalloped border was Tori's idea, and the color scheme was totally her choice. She helped envision a quilting pattern which reflected her temperament—no fussy, frilly flourishes. My role here was one of technical adviser. In all other aspects, this is truly *Tori's Star.*

Skill Level:
Patchwork—Intermediate
Scalloped Border—Advanced
Quilting—Intermediate (curved lines)

Approximate Finished Size: 76″ x 95″
Number of Blocks and Finished Block Size:
12 Blocks—16″ x 16″ each

Materials:

COLOR OF FABRIC	YARDS REQUIRED	TEMPLATE REQUIRED	NUMBER TO CUT	NUMBER USED PER BLOCK
Pink	2¼	20	24	2
		20F*	24	2
		41	24	2
		41F*	24	2
Blue	2¼	14	12	1
		53	96	8
Gray	1	21	24	2
		21F*	24	2
		53	48	4
White	5	14	48	4
		18	48	4
		41	96	8
		51	48	4
		53	96	8
Joining Strips: White	**	2″ x 16″***	8	—
		2″ x 52″***	3	—
Border: Blue	**	1″ x 52″***	2	—
		1″ x 72″***	2	—
White	**	10″ x 72″***	2	—
		10″ x 74″***	2	—
Bias Strip: Pink	**	1½″ wide	—	—
Binding: Blue	**	2½″ wide	—	—
Backing: White Cotton or Muslin	6	—	—	—

*—Flip or turn over template if fabric is one-sided.
**—Yardage is included in above measurement.
***—Measurements are given without seam allowance.

Block Assembly:

Each block contains 3 different sections. Join pieces and sections as indicated by the diagrams. Make 12 blocks.

Block Sections

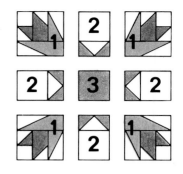

Section 1—Make 2 as shown and 2 the mirror image of these.

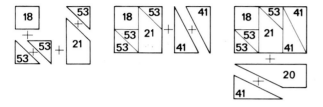

Section 2—Make 4.

Section 3—Template 14.

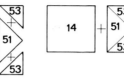

Final Assembly: Join sections into columns, rotating blocks as shown. Join the 3 columns.

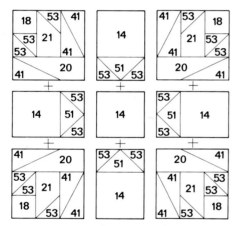

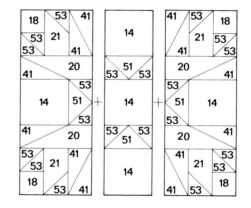

Quilt Top Assembly:

Row Assembly—Alternate 3 blocks with two 16″ joining strips and join as shown. Make 4 rows.

Center Section—Alternate 4 rows with three 52″ joining strips and join as shown.

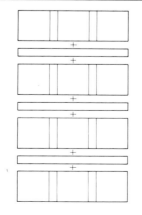

120

Border Assembly—Join 1″ x 52″ strips to top and bottom of work. Then join 1″ x 72″ strips to each side.

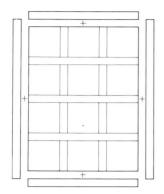

Join 10″ x 72″ strips to sides and 10″ x 74″ strips to top and bottom.

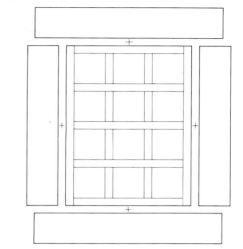

Scalloped Border:

Draw a guideline for scallop template 9″ from the seam line of the 1″ border strip. (See Scalloped Border Diagram. Scallop pattern can be found in Pattern Section.) Start at the center of the sides and draw scallops, rounding corners and proceeding across the bottom edge. The pattern will center on the bottom edge in the same way it does on the sides. Leave the top edge straight. Cut scallops along guidelines. Attach 1½″ pink bias strip to scalloped edges. Don't worry if it looks bulky at this point.

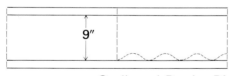

Scalloped Border Diagram

Quilting:

Outline-quilt ¼″ inside seams of star pieces. Quilting lines for white areas are drawn from one seam junction to the other. (See Quilting Diagram.)

Refer to Quilting Diagram for Scalloped Border. Quilt in-the-ditch where bias strip is attached. Quilt on bias strip ¾″ from ditch quilting. Curved parallel quilting lines are 1″ apart and 1¾″ from ditch quilting. Parallel quilting lines near the

1″ border strip are 1¼″ apart and ¼″ from seam.

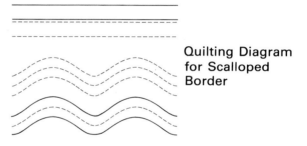

Quilting Diagram for Scalloped Border

Finished Edges:

Along scalloped edge *only*, trim away excess of *all* layers to ¼″ from quilting line. Use this quilting line, which will be hidden in binding seam, as a guideline for attaching binding. Bind with a double-fold, 1¼″-wide bias strip.

Counterpoint

Counterpoint is a musical term. It refers to a style, and a technique of composition used to achieve that style. Contrapuntal music employs multiple melodies, set against each other, moving along together. What does it sound like? If you like Bach, you like counterpoint. What does it look like? This quilt is a suggestion of the visual effect of playing two fabric melodies against each other.

Skill Level:
    Patchwork—Beginner
    Quilting—Beginner
Finished Size: 54″ x 72″
Number of Blocks and
Finished Block Size:
    12 Blocks—18″ x 18″ each

Materials:

COLOR OF FABRIC	YARDS REQUIRED	TEMPLATE REQUIRED	NUMBER TO CUT	NUMBER USED PER BLOCK
Blue	1¼	16	48	4
		46	72	6
Orange	1	46	96	8
Print	1	34	24	2
		50	48	4
White	2½	16	96	8
		34	24	2
		46	168	14
Binding: Orange	¾	—	—	—
Backing: White Cotton or Muslin	4	—	—	—

Block Assembly:

Each block contains 2 sections. Join pieces and sections as indicated by the diagrams. Make 12 blocks.

Block Sections

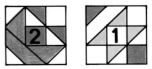

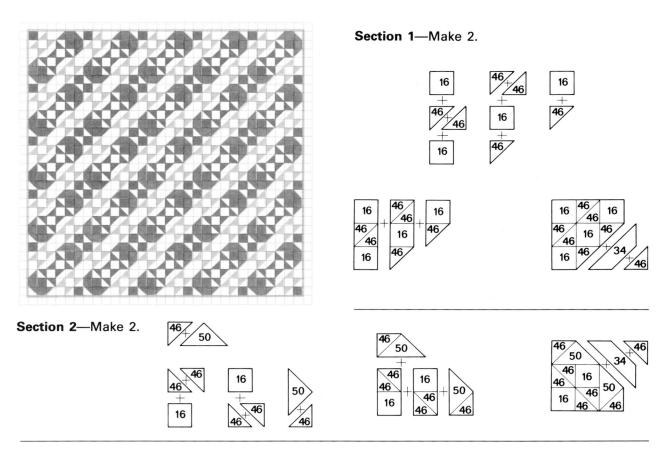

Section 1—Make 2.

Section 2—Make 2.

Final Assembly: Join, rotating sections as shown. Arrow indicates top of the block. Make 4 rows of 3 blocks each, keeping them all right side up. (See Whole Quilt Diagram.)

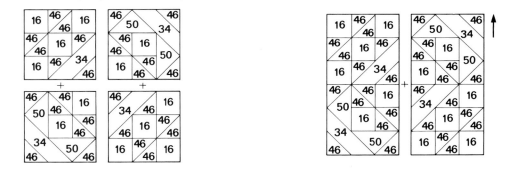

Quilting:
Outline-quilt ¼″ from seams.

Finished Edges:
Bind raw edges with orange fabric.

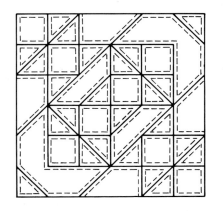

123

A-Maze-Ment

This quilt is just for fun—a fabric puzzle with no solution. Hang it on the wall as a conversation piece, or lay it on the floor so that toddlers can explore its pattern of bright colors. Beginning quilters will enjoy its easy patchwork, simple outline quilting, and small size. To your a-maze-ment, you'll have a quilt to be proud of in no time.

Skill Level:
  Patchwork—Beginner
  Quilting—Beginner
Finished Size: 60″ x 60″
Number of Blocks and Finished Block Size:
  14 Block A—10″ x 10″ each
  14 Block B—10″ x 10″ each
   4 Block C—10″ x 10″ each
   4 Block D—10″ x 10″ each

Materials:

COLOR OF FABRIC	YARDS REQUIRED	TEMPLATE REQUIRED	NUMBER TO CUT	NUMBER USED PER			
				BLOCK A	BLOCK B	BLOCK C	BLOCK D
Rust	2½	3	28	1	1	—	—
		7	18	1	—	1	—
		8	36	1	1	2	—
		9	44	1	1	1	3
		18	28	1	1	—	—
Green	2½	3	28	1	1	—	—
		7	18	—	1	—	1
		8	36	1	1	—	2
		9	44	1	1	3	1
		18	28	1	1	—	—
Binding: Rust	½	—	—	—	—	—	—
Backing: Rust	3¾	—	—	—	—	—	—

Block Assembly:

Blocks A and B are pieced in exactly the same way and differ only in color placement. Blocks C and D are pieced in exactly the same way and differ only in color placement.

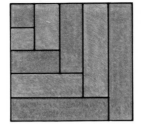

Block A

Blocks A and B—Make 14 of each block for a total of 28 blocks. Color placement for Block B is the exact opposite of Block A.

Block Assembly Order for Block A and Block B:

    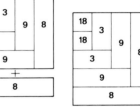 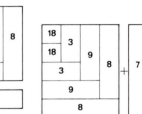

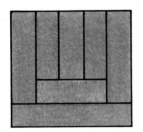

Block C

Blocks C and D—Make 4 of each block for a total of 8 blocks. Color placement for Block D is the exact opposite of Block C.

Block Assembly Order for Block C and Block D:

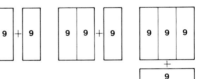

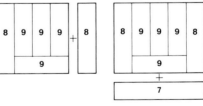

Quilt Assembly:

Join blocks into 6 rows of 6 blocks each, according to Setting Diagram. Refer to Whole Quilt Diagram for proper block rotation.

Quilting and Finished Edges:

Outline-quilt ¼″ from all seams. Bind raw edges with rust fabric.

Setting Diagram

A	B	A	B	A	B
B	A	D	C	B	A
A	D	A	B	C	B
B	C	B	A	D	A
A	B	C	D	A	B
B	A	B	A	B	A

Illusion

The illusion here is movement—movement created partly by the pattern and partly by the colors. For maximum effect, use two contrasting colors, the bolder the better.

Though this pattern is not really difficult, it does have a lot of pieces to cut and sew and lots of quilting! It's likely to be an overwhelming quilt for the beginner in terms of time. Don't be deceived by the fact that there are only nine blocks. Each one of them is large and has oodles of triangles.

Skill Level:
Patchwork—Intermediate
Quilting—Intermediate
Finished Size: 90″ x 90″
Number of Blocks and Finished Block Size:
9 Blocks—30″ x 30″ each

Block Assembly:
Each block contains two each of Sections 1 and 2. Join pieces and sections as indicated by the diagrams. Make 9 blocks.

Materials:

COLOR OF FABRIC	YARDS REQUIRED	TEMPLATE REQUIRED	NUMBER TO CUT	NUMBER USED PER BLOCK
Green	5	28 extend to 17″	18	2
		32	72	8
		34	18	2
		46	540	60
Pink	3	28 extend to 12¾″	18	2
		28 extend to 21¼″	18	2
		32	108	12
		46	18	2
White	3	46	450	50
Binding: Green	¾	—	—	—
Backing: White Cotton or Muslin	6	—	—	—

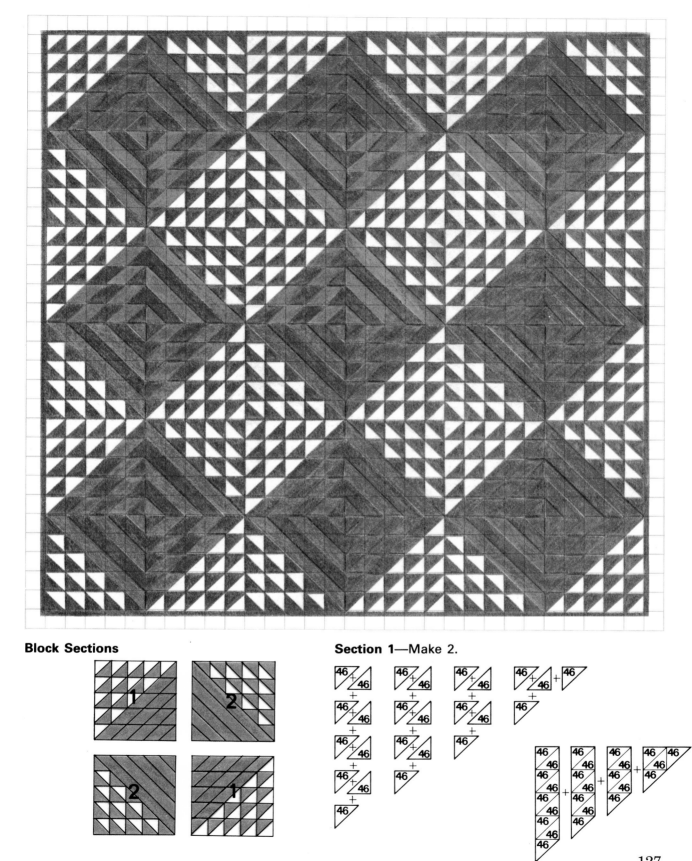

Block Sections

Section 1—Make 2.

127

Section 1—continued

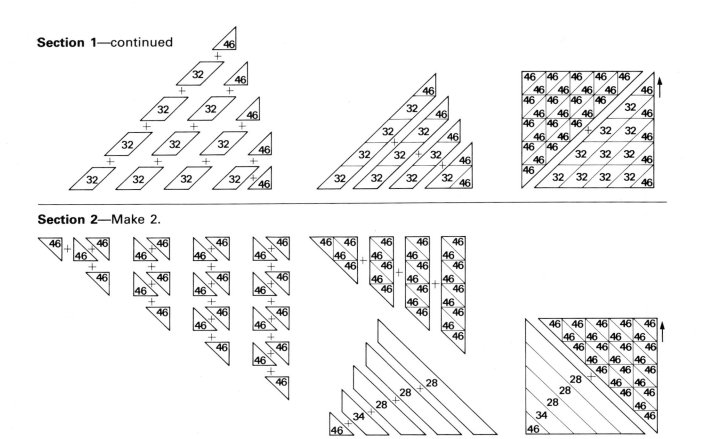

Section 2—Make 2.

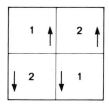

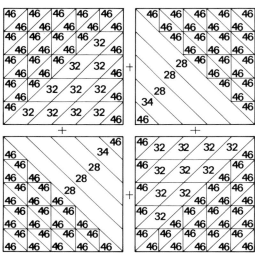

Final Assembly: Join sections, rotating them as indicated on Block Setting Diagram. Set blocks right side up in 3 rows of 3 blocks each. (See Whole Quilt Diagram.) Join rows.

Block Setting Diagram

Quilting:
Outline-quilt ¼″ from all seams. Quilt parallel lines ¼″ apart in white triangles.

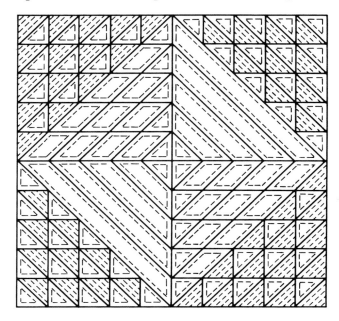

Finished Edges:
Bind raw edges with green fabric.

Dominoes

We all love to watch the toppling of a row of dominoes. It's a simple game with endless variations, especially enjoyable on a rainy day. This quilt, too, is a simple game with potential variations. Beginners will have no problem with this pattern, and it could even be used for a child's first experiment in quiltmaking. Lots of quilting dresses up its simplicity, but the alternate quilting diagram is recommended if this is your very first quilt.

Skill Level:
Patchwork—Beginner
Quilting—Intermediate (large amount of straight-line and outline)
—Beginner (Alternate Quilting Diagram)
Finished Size: 84″ x 84″
Number of Blocks and Finished Block Size:
28 Blocks—21″ x 12″ each

Materials:

COLOR OF FABRIC	YARDS REQUIRED	TEMPLATE REQUIRED	NUMBER TO CUT	NUMBER USED PER BLOCK
Pink Gingham*	1¼	16	112	4
Green	2	16	112	4
		50	56	2
Print	1	50	56	2
Pink	4¼	1	112	4
		22 extend to 9″	56	2
		32	28	1
		46	112	4
Binding: Pink	¾	—	—	—
Backing: White Cotton or Muslin	5¾	—	—	—

*—See Working with Gingham on next page.

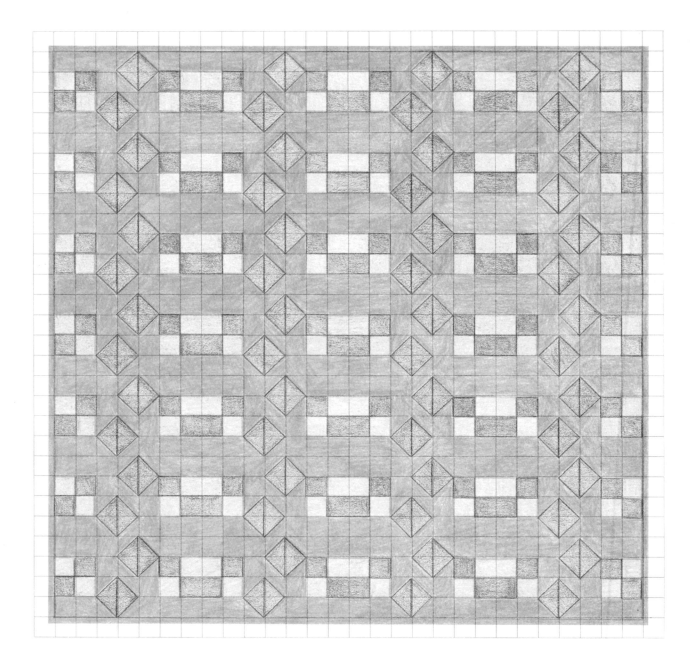

Working with Gingham:

Gingham is not a particularly easy fabric to work with in quiltmaking. Its use in this quilt seemed necessary to evoke the childhood memories associated with dominoes. Keep the following in mind when using gingham:

1. Almost all gingham is produced in poly/cotton blends. Since these blends do not tear straight with the grain, gingham must be cut rather than torn.

2. Gingham should be cut according to its pattern and works best for squares.

3. Try to avoid inexpensive fabrics in which the pattern is not woven straight or is printed only on the top of the fabric.

130

Block Assembly:

Each block contains 2 sections. Join pieces and sections according to the diagram. Make 28 blocks.

Block Sections

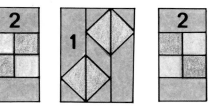

Section 1

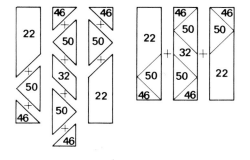

Section 2—Make 2 for each block. One Section 2 is the mirror image of the other.

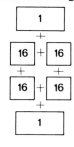

Final Assembly: Join a Section 2 to each side of Section 1 as shown. Make 7 rows of 4 blocks each. Refer to Whole Quilt Diagram and join rows.

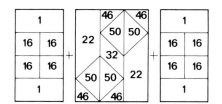

Quilting:

Outline-quilt ¼″ from seams of squares and triangles. For the remainder of quilting, parallel quilting lines are ¼″ apart.

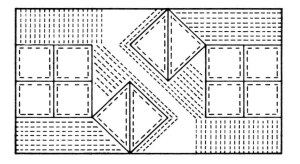

For Alternate Quilting Diagram— Outline-quilt ¼″ from all seams. The quilting line that zig-zags between the two large diamonds is ¾″ from the outline quilting. The quilting line that runs parallel with the quilting line along the top edge of the block is 1¼″ from it. The same is true for the quilting line along the bottom edge of the block.

Finished Edges:

Bind raw edges with pink fabric.

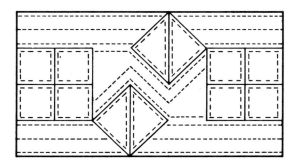

Patterns for Templates

These patterns include all the shapes you will need to piece any of the quilts in this book. The materials chart (appearing with the instructions for each quilt) will give the template numbers required for that quilt, any extension measurements, and template placement information. Pattern pieces are numbered consecutively in this section, and arrows represent crosswise grain lines. *Remember to add ¼″ seam allowance to all pattern pieces.*

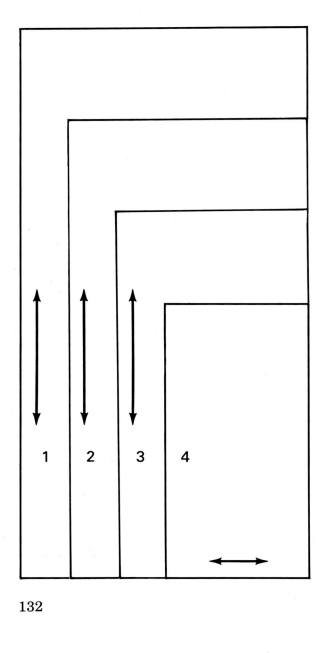

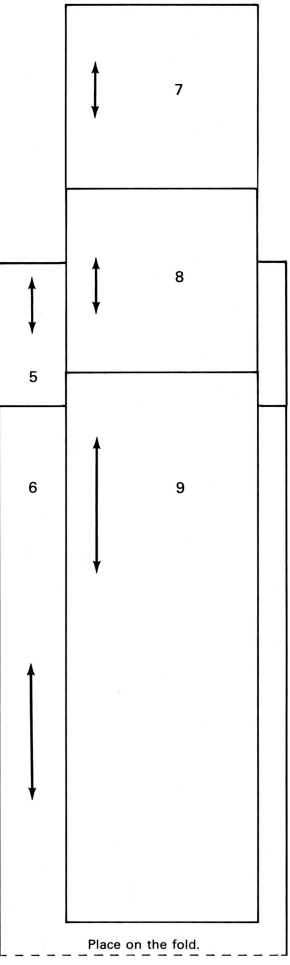

Place on the fold.

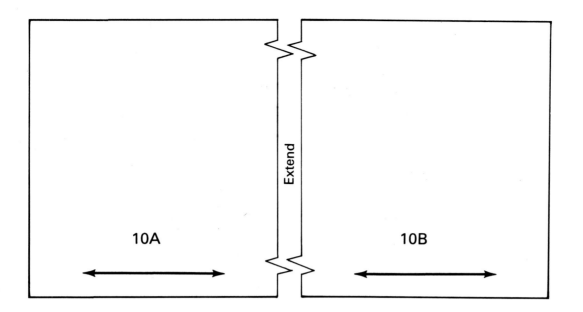

10A   Extend   10B

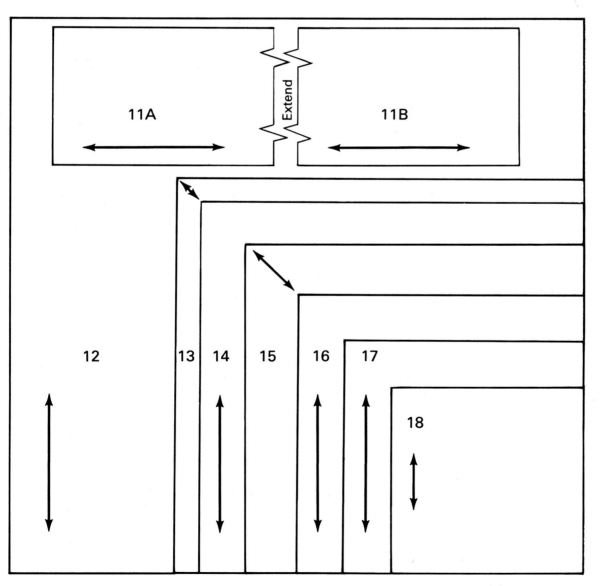

11A   Extend   11B

12   13   14   15   16   17   18

133

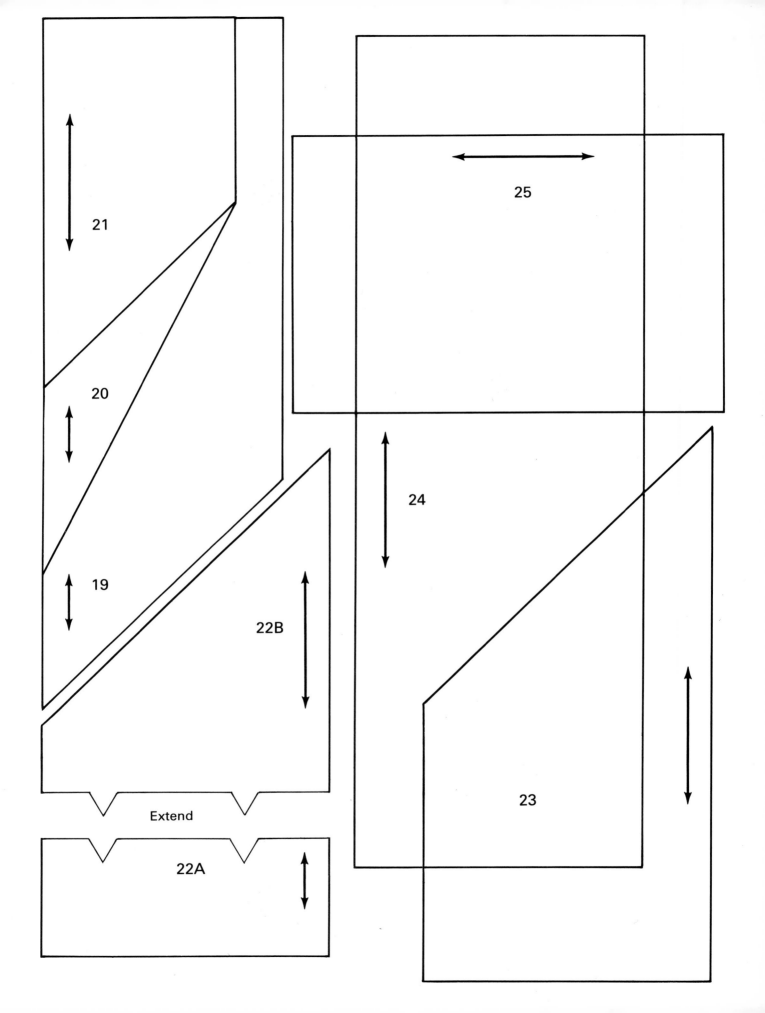

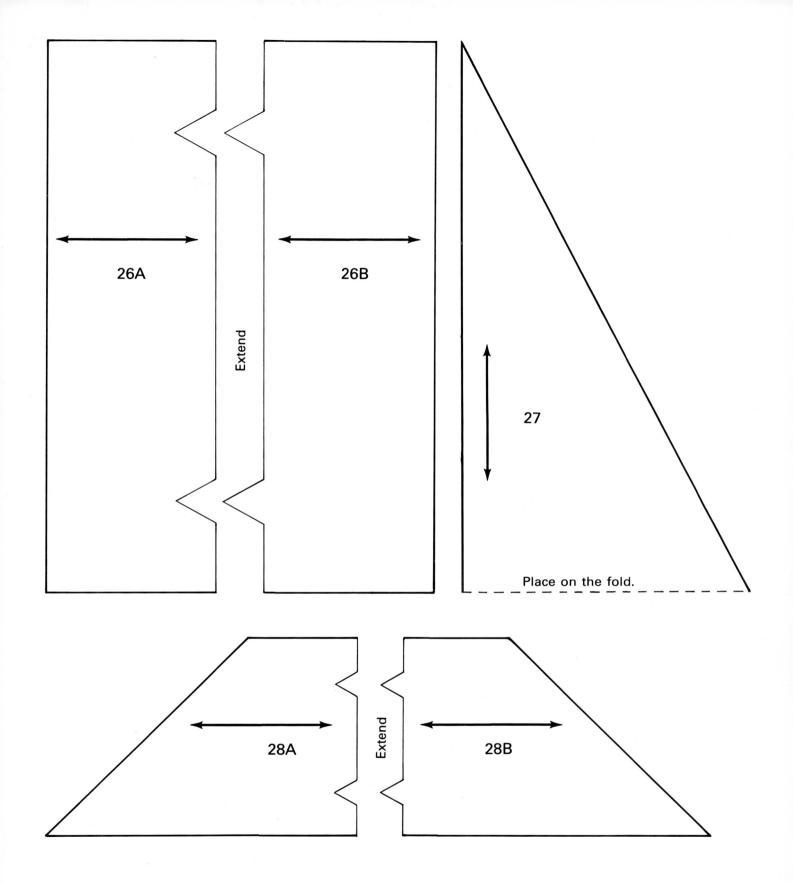

26A

26B

Extend

27

Place on the fold.

28A

Extend

28B

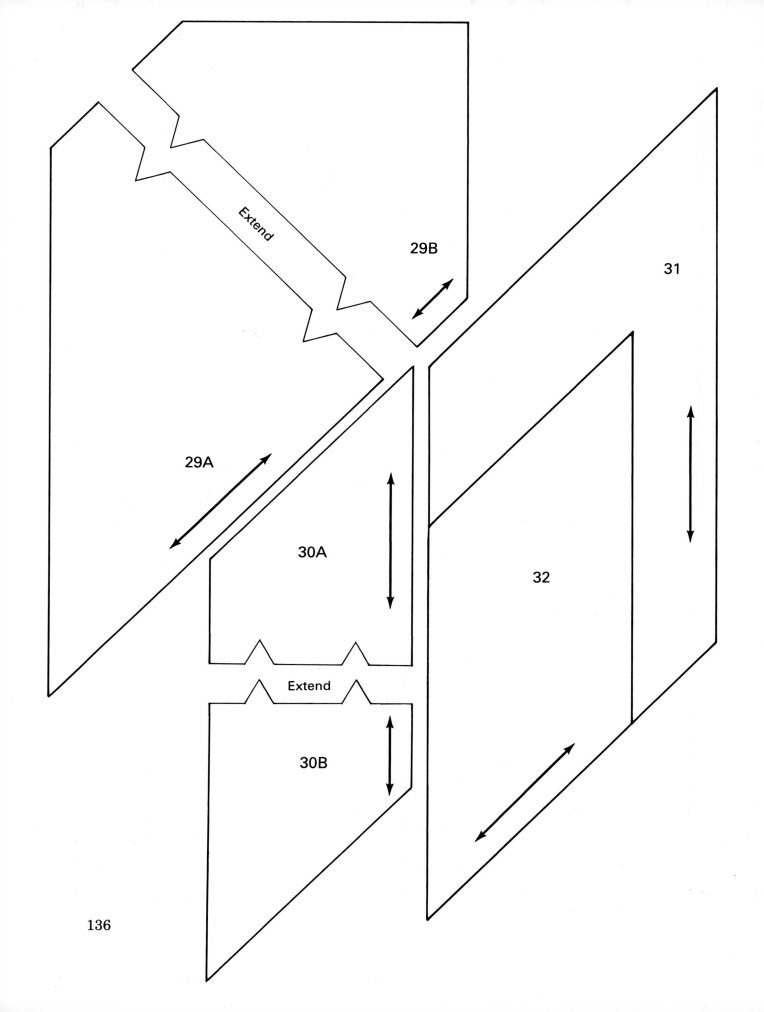

29B

Extend

31

29A

30A

32

Extend

30B

136

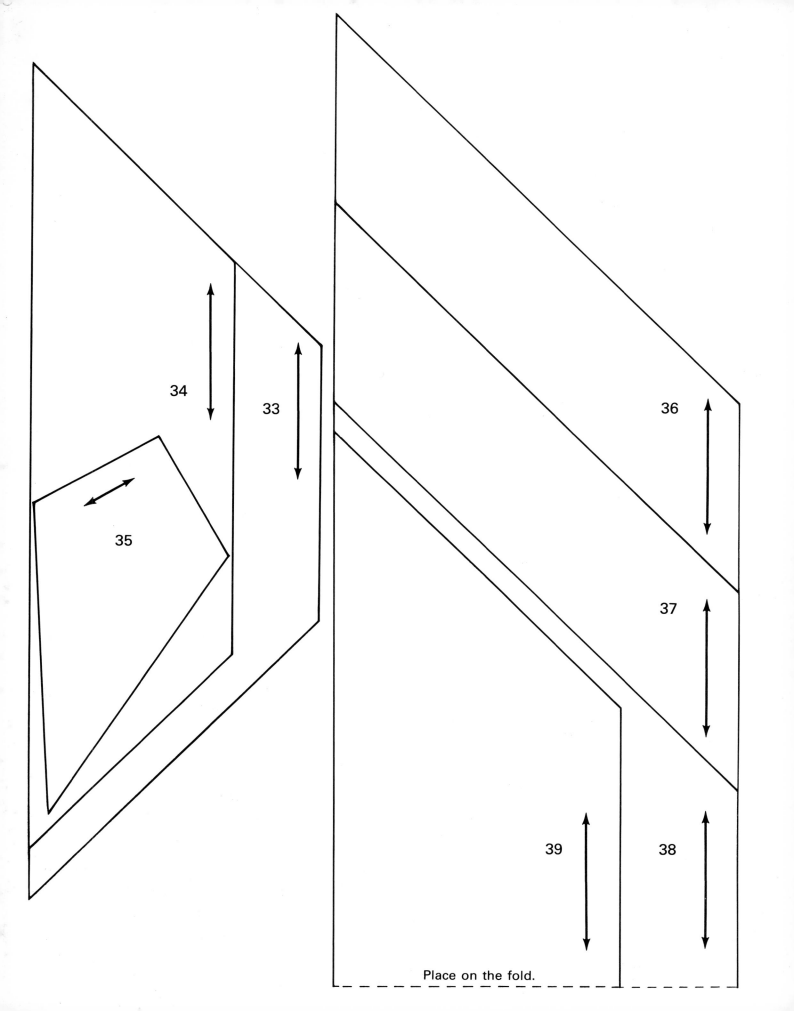

34

33

35

36

37

39 38

Place on the fold.

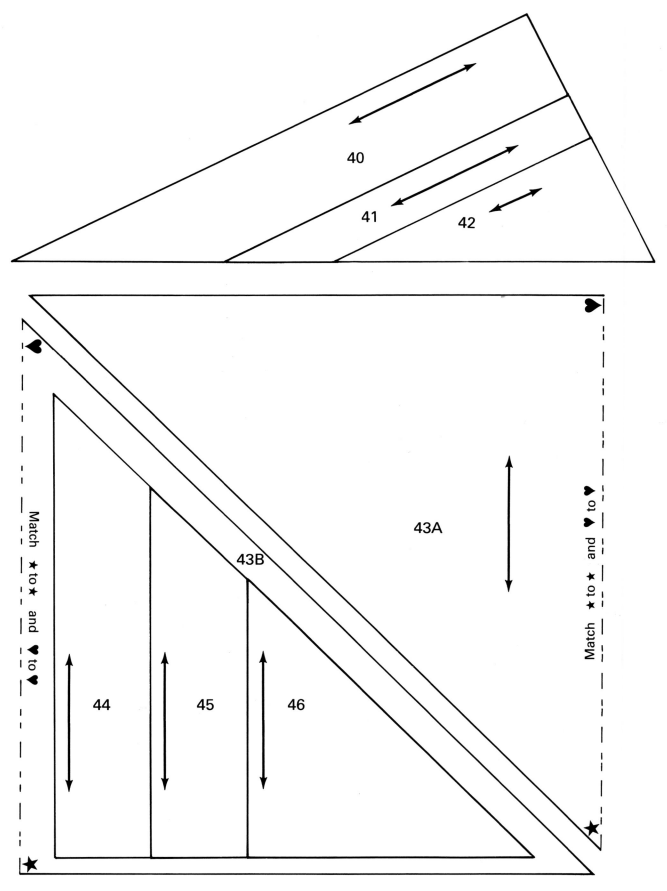

40

41

42

43A

43B

Match ★ to ★ and ♥ to ♥

Match ★ to ★ and ♥ to ♥

44

45

46

138

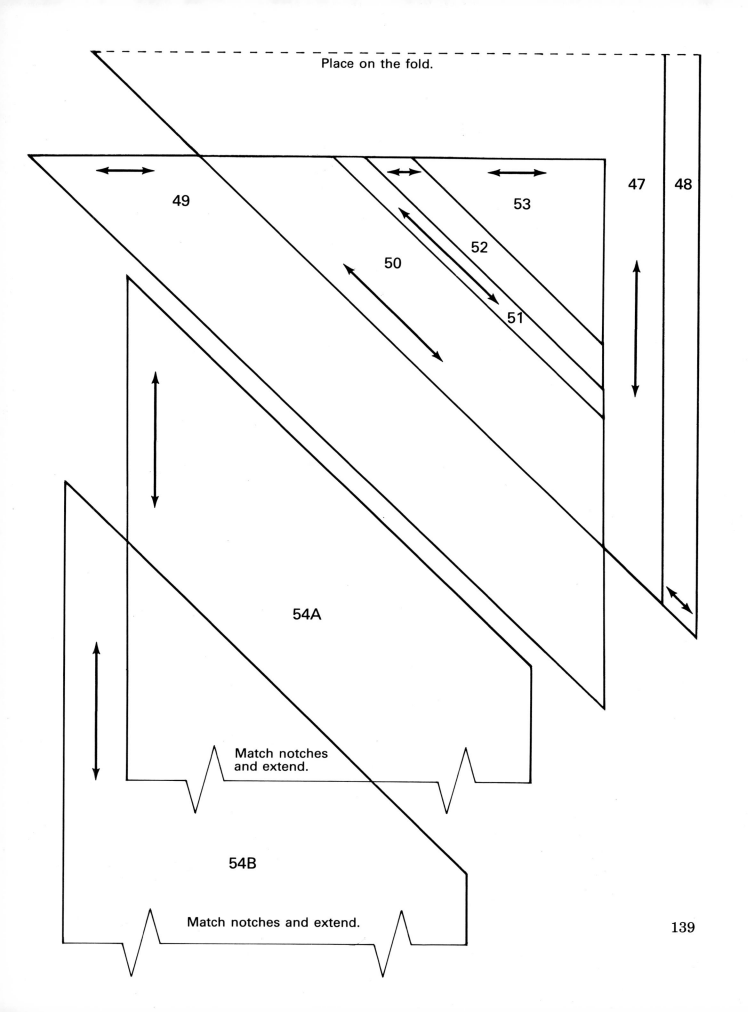

Place on the fold.

47   48

49

53

52

50

51

54A

54B

Match notches and extend.

Match notches and extend.

139

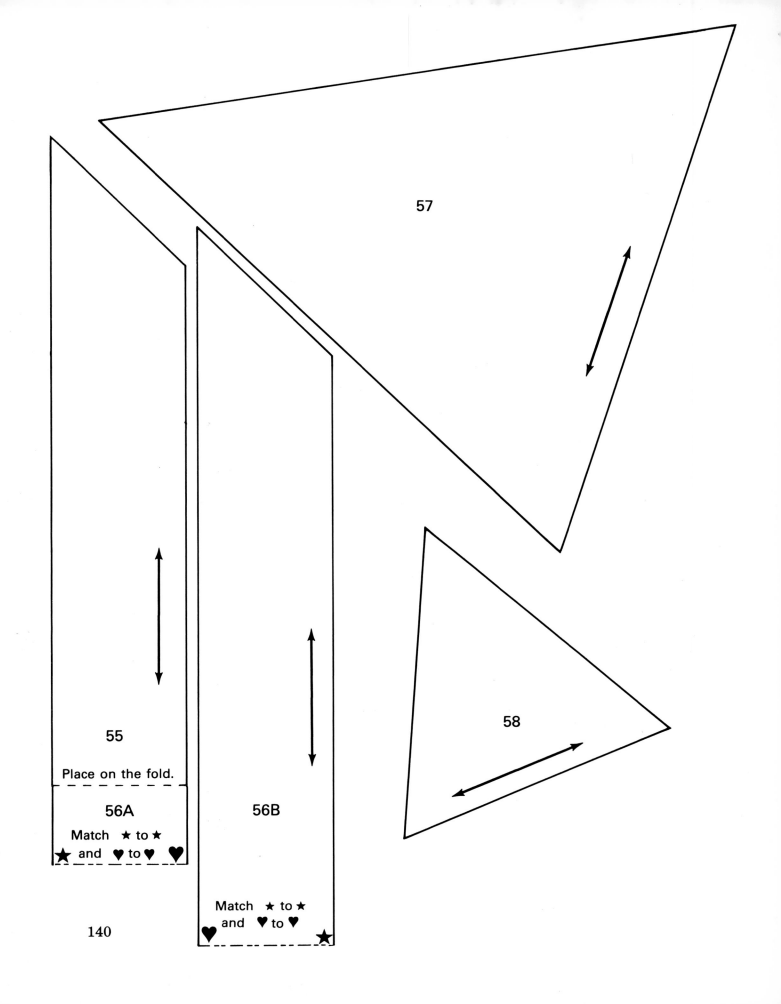

57

55

Place on the fold.

56A

Match ★ to ★
and ♥ to ♥

140

56B

Match ★ to ★
and ♥ to ♥

58

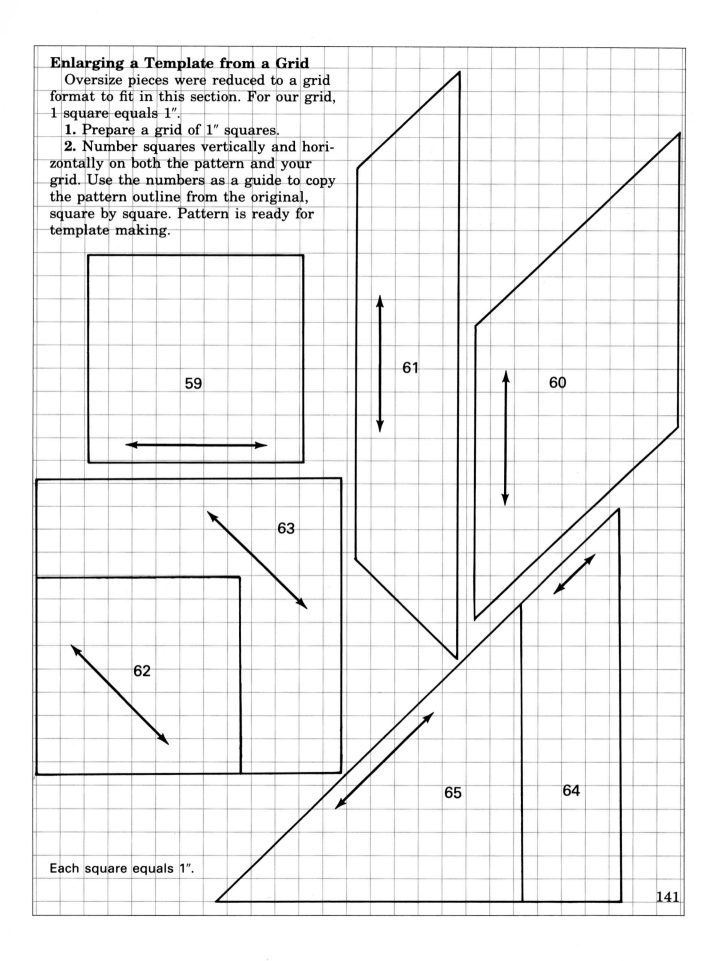

Enlarging a Template from a Grid

Oversize pieces were reduced to a grid format to fit in this section. For our grid, 1 square equals 1″.

1. Prepare a grid of 1″ squares.

2. Number squares vertically and horizontally on both the pattern and your grid. Use the numbers as a guide to copy the pattern outline from the original, square by square. Pattern is ready for template making.

59

61

60

63

62

65

64

Each square equals 1″.

141

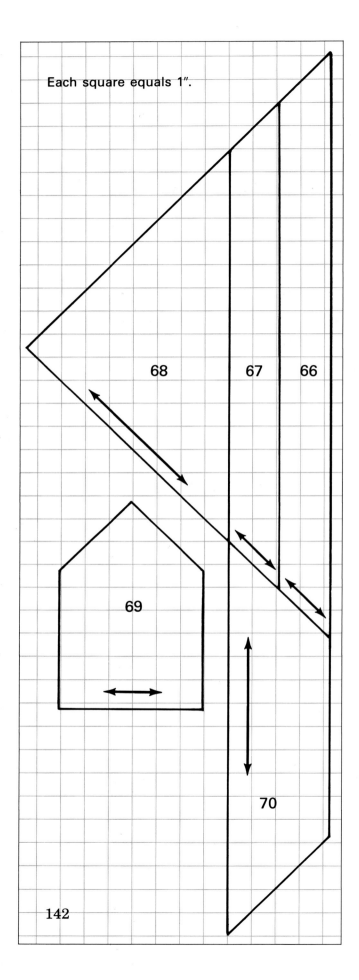

Each square equals 1".

68

67

66

69

70

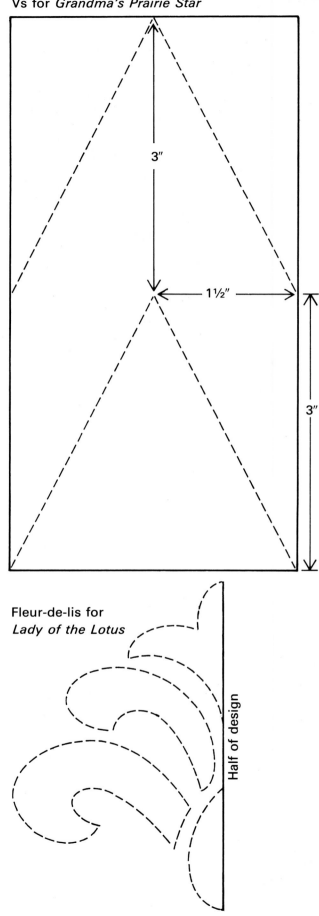

Vs for *Grandma's Prairie Star*

3"

1½"

3"

Fleur-de-lis for
Lady of the Lotus

Half of design

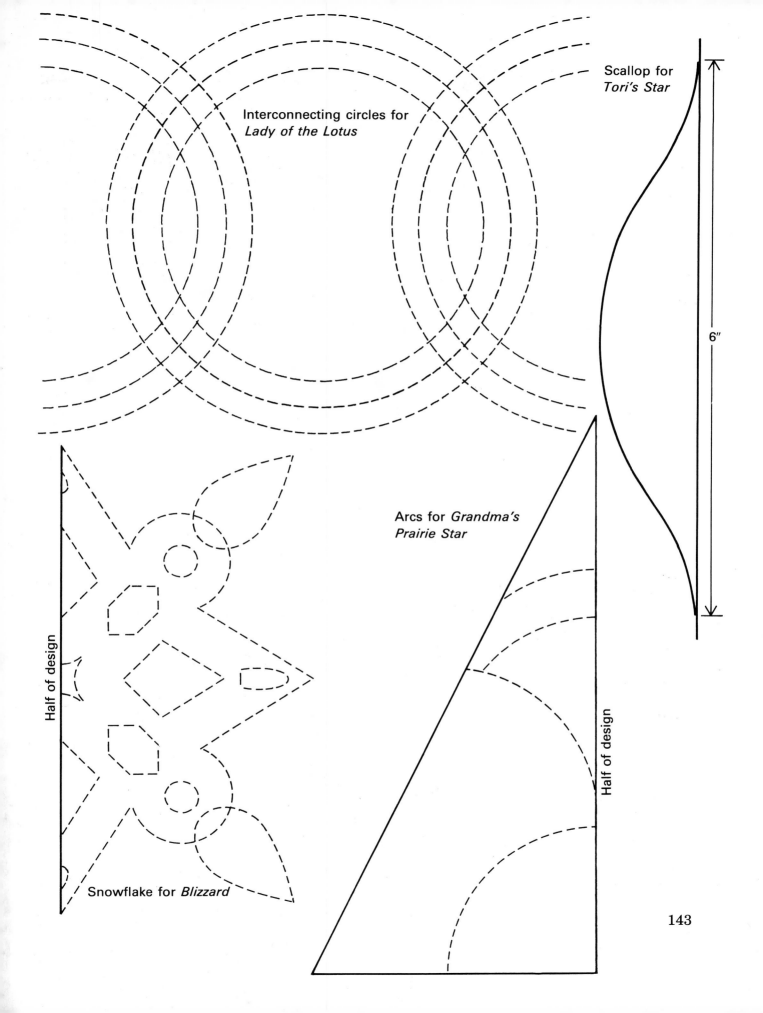

Interconnecting circles for *Lady of the Lotus*

Scallop for *Tori's Star*

6"

Arcs for *Grandma's Prairie Star*

Half of design

Half of design

Snowflake for *Blizzard*

143

CREATIVE IDEAS FOR LIVING™

THE Creative Lifestyle Magazine

12 issues, $13.95.*

YOU'RE

active in career, family and leisure time
energetic in your outlook
creative in your approach

CREATIVE IDEAS FOR LIVING™ is for you!

CREATIVE IDEAS FOR LIVING™ is as individual as you are. The perfect guide to expanding a lifestyle that sparkles with freshness and vitality.

CREATIVE IDEAS FOR LIVING™ helps you live more beautifully—for less. Less time, less wasted energy, less complication.

The ideas of our editors and other creative women across the country show you how to develop and expand your own unique style in everything you do. The advice, instructions, and photographs are all geared to make you the most creative you can be!

To receive CREATIVE IDEAS FOR LIVING **each month, simply write to:**

CREATIVE IDEAS FOR LIVING
Box C-30 ● Birmingham, AL 35283

* Rate good in United States. Canada, U.S. Possessions, and Foreign: $16.00 per year.